THE 5 FUNDAMENTALS OF BUILDING A RETIREMENT PORTFOLIO

THE FINANCIAL LEXICON

"Be concerned only with the pure truth in what you read and not with the greatness or lack of learning of the author. Think more of what is said than of the one who said it."

Thomas à Kempis

Table of Contents

Why Publish Under a Pseudonym?

There are a few reasons I write under a pseudonym. First, I am of the opinion that neither academic nor professional distinctions make an individual a successful investor. I believe the investing community as a whole would be better served by focusing more time on the merits of an idea or investment thesis rather than simply assigning merit to an idea or investment thesis because of who said it or wrote it. Publishing under a pseudonym is my way of reinforcing that belief, as it allows the attention to be diverted away from me, the person behind the pseudonym, and shifts the reader's focus exclusively to the topics discussed in this book.

Second, I am not seeking fame from my writing. I am not trying to win anyone's business, and I am not trying to sell any financial products. I am hoping to help people think through the process of building a retirement portfolio so that each person, whether individually or together with a financial advisor, will feel reasonably confident in his or her ability to judge whether a particular asset is right for his or her portfolio.

Also, what I write is not intended to act as investment advice. I am currently not interested in acting as either a financial advisor or a portfolio manager. Instead, I am more interested in presenting ideas and new ways of thinking through investing-related issues in an attempt to help individuals become the best informed investors they can be. Whether you choose to manage your own money or have an advisor manage it for you, I hope this book helps you attain a better understanding of the financial assets available to you and what questions to think about when deciding whether certain assets should find a home in your portfolio.

A Note to Readers

Whether you are an everyday investor interested in the financial markets or an experienced financial professional looking for new insights into portfolio construction and various assets, I hope you will find this book useful. If you are an investor with less experience in the financial markets, I suggest reading this book from start to finish in the order it was written. If you are a financial professional well-versed in the various assets available to the income-oriented investor, you may want to skip Chapters 2, 3, and 4.

One exception is the municipal bond subsection in Chapter 4. Regardless of your investing prowess, I think it will be worthwhile to read the part about calculating the taxable-equivalent yield of a municipal bond. The content of the discussion may surprise you.

In general, the first four chapters of the book are more informational than thought-provoking. Thereafter, I hope you will find the book both informational *and* thought-provoking.

Introduction

Picture this: It is your retirement day. You are filled with mixed emotions of jubilation and nervousness. As you walk out of your place of employment for the final time, you realize your life is about to change forever. You will shed certain responsibilities and stresses, but you will acquire new responsibilities and stresses.

You will no longer receive that reliable, steady, and predictable payment for the services you provided to your employers over the course of your working life. The manner in which you grew accustomed to thinking about income throughout your life will change forever the moment you say goodbye to your employer for the last time. This is a very big deal.

Instead of a world in which you perform a task or service and are compensated a relatively short time later, you will enter a world in which you will rely on promises from the government in the form of Social Security, promises from an employer in the form of a pension, or income from your investment portfolio in order to meet your needs and wants over the remaining years of your life.

In order to more confidently enter the exciting phase of your life called "retirement," it is essential to have a solid, well-thought-through and well-executed retirement plan. Every one of us can cut our expenses to the bone, but without income, what we once viewed as bare minimum expenses will suddenly feel like the weight of the Titanic dragging us down.

Managing expenses throughout one's life, including during retirement, is a unique undertaking with a variety of factors. It is virtually impossible for anyone, whether a financial planner or a friend giving you advice, to accurately predict exactly how you will spend your money in retirement. While managing expenses will certainly be extremely important for most people in retirement, this book focuses on the five fundamentals needed to build a well-rounded retirement portfolio.

If you have spent any time scouring publications on retirement planning, you likely discovered that there is an abundance of literature focused on telling people how their money should be allocated in retirement and how the retirement portfolio should be drawn down. The focus is often centered on a specific allocation across equities, fixed income, and cash, as well as a discussion on the percentage a portfolio should be drawn down each year to ensure maximum sustainability of one's money. This book will take a different approach.

Instead of diving right in and telling you exactly what you should buy for your portfolio without any knowledge of your risk tolerance, time horizons, or investment objectives, this book will outline a variety of investments to consider. It will also include an abundance of questions and ideas you should think through as you decide which investments best suit your needs. In addition, it will help you work through the process of figuring out the asset allocation that is right for your portfolio.

From a risk tolerance perspective, did the inflation experiences of the 1970s and early 1980s shape your views of investing such that fixed income will simply never be a major part of your portfolio? Perhaps the two declines of more than 50% in the S&P 500 between 2000 and 2009 molded your view of equities in such a way that anything more than a minimal allocation to stocks makes you uncomfortable.

In terms of time horizons, rather than simply focusing on standard life expectancies, as many advisors might be tempted to do in a publication on building a retirement portfolio, a more in-depth plan would build in one's prior personal and familial medical history as a guide for life expectancy. It might even attempt to model the likelihood of medical breakthroughs increasing life expectancy.

Understanding your investment objectives is also important. Are you hoping to spend your last penny on your final day of life, or do you hope to bequeath a remaining portion of the investment portfolio?

All this information is important and necessary when building a strategy for your retirement portfolio. For investors using financial advisors, this can all be discussed in detail during meetings with the advisors. For those taking a self-directed approach, you can think about all this valuable information as you move along in the planning process.

But first, before deciding specifically in what to invest or listening to someone else tell you how to invest your retirement money, it is important to understand the different elements of building a retirement portfolio. Therefore, rather than telling you how your money should be invested in retirement or how much you should draw it down over time, I hope you will find it useful to focus on the things you should *think about* when constructing your retirement portfolio.

It can take years to build the ideal retirement portfolio, and even after you "finish," you will likely have to make changes over time. By learning about the variety of investment options available to you and the various questions you should consider when investing in certain assets, you will arm yourself with the knowledge to make intelligent, well-thought-out decisions along your investing journey. This will be far more valuable to you in the long run than someone's giving you the same old spiel about a supposed one-size-fits-all formula for allocating and drawing down your assets. The truth is, there is no one-size-fits-all investment recipe and no magic formula for how to make it through retirement. Each person's situation is unique and requires careful attention.

Understanding the various aspects of building a retirement portfolio is important not only for self-directed retirement investors but also for individuals relying on financial advisors to manage their portfolios. In order to feel as comfortable as possible in your retirement investments, you should have a good grasp of the decision-making process behind those selections. Inherent in that decision-making process should be the following five fundamentals: predictable income, inflation protection, deflation protection, liquidity, and principal preservation.

Let's explore each one!

I

Part I

Predictable Income

As you know, in order to make it through retirement, you will need income. In order to make it through retirement with a higher level of financial certainty than you otherwise would have, a *predictable* income stream is extremely important. By predictable income, I am referring to income that is paid to you on a regular schedule and can be relied upon to continually arrive under normal as well as most adverse conditions.

It is important not to confuse predictable income with a guarantee of income. Contrary to what you might hear, there are no guarantees in the financial world. You can achieve reasonable safety and security in your portfolio. You can even create a portfolio that can withstand tremendous stresses. But one thing you cannot do is create guaranteed income. Understanding this is of great importance. Even assets that conventional wisdom holds are "risk free" do have risks.

How does one obtain predictable income? There are a variety of ways, including annuities, dividends from equities or equity-like investments, and fixed income products. There are also means of obtaining predictable income in retirement that are not part of a traditional investment portfolio. Some people might be fortunate enough to have employer-sponsored pensions; others might receive rental income from real estate they own. For those who would enjoy a "working retirement," a part-time job or hobby might also be a source of income. This part of the book begins by taking a look at two other sources of predictable income on which millions of Americans rely: Social Security and Railroad Retirement benefits.

Chapter 1

Social Security

and

Railroad Retirement Benefits

What is commonly referred to as "Social Security" is officially known as the "Federal Old-Age, Survivors, and Disability Insurance Benefits" (OASDI). Social Security is a type of income that is well known and widely written about; a wealth of information on this program can be found at ssa.gov, the website of the United States Social Security Administration (SSA). Social Security was created under the Social Security Act, signed into law by President Franklin D. Roosevelt on August 14, 1935. Specifically, "Title II – Federal Old-Age, Survivors, and Disability Insurance Benefits" of the Social Security Act provides details for the program commonly referred to as "Social Security." Title II was originally called "Federal Old-Age Benefits."

OASDI was not the only program receiving funds under the Social Security Act of 1935, and additional programs have since been added to the social welfare system in the United States. In addition to federal old-age benefits, the Social Security Act of 1935 provided grants to states to assist with other aid programs. Title III provided grants for unemployment compensation. Title IV provided grants for "needy dependent children" (the language has since been changed). Title V provided grants for services "promoting the health of mothers and children" (the language has since been changed). Title VI, which was repealed in 2004, was originally called "Public Health Work," providing federal funds for "assisting States, counties, health districts, and other political subdivisions of the States in establishing and maintaining adequate public-health services." And Title X provided grants for helping blind people. Since 1935, additional Titles were added to the Act, bringing the total to twenty-one from the original eleven.

Today, we have a multitude of additional state and federally administered programs, including: the National School Lunch Program (established in 1946); the Special Milk Program (1954); the Supplemental Nutrition Assistance Program, better known as food stamps (1939, 1964); Medicare (1965); Medicaid (1965); the School Breakfast Program (1966); Supplemental Security Income (1974); the Low Income Home Energy Assistance Program (1981); Temporary Assistance for Needy Families (1996); and the Fresh Fruit and Vegetable Program (2002). There are two years listed for food stamps because the first Food Stamp Program was a temporary program that ran from 1939 to 1943. The Food Stamp Act of 1964 made the Food Stamp Program permanent. On October 1, 2008, the name of the program was changed to the Supplemental Nutrition Assistance Program, also known as SNAP.

Although the modern-day social welfare system has its roots in the 1930s, the use of taxation to provide relief to those in need dates back to colonial times. According to the "Pre-Social Security Period" section of SSA's "Historical Background and Development of Social Security," the first colonial "poor laws" were modeled after the English Poor Law of 1601. Under that law, taxes were levied to fund programs, but relief activities were administered at the community level rather than at the national level. Among other things, receiving aid both in colonial America and during the early decades of the United States could subject a person to loss of personal property and loss of voting rights.

The first national pension program for soldiers, which provided limited pensions to veterans, was signed in 1776. In 1862, the Civil War Pension program was signed into law, providing disability benefits to soldiers and benefits to widows and orphans of deceased soldiers. By 1894, a whopping 37% of the federal budget was going toward military pension payments. In 1906, old-age benefits were added for Civil War veterans. Given that Civil War pensions could be inherited by widows of veterans, it was not unusual for elderly veterans to attract young wives. And that leads to this shocking fact: According to the Social Security Administration, the last Civil War pension payment to a surviving widow of a Civil War veteran was paid in 1999. That is 134 years after the end of the Civil War!

Along with establishing the Social Security Act, in the 1930s, Congress established a Railroad Retirement system, administered by the Railroad Retirement Board (RRB), which provided benefits to railroad employees. The Railroad Retirement Act of 1934, later deemed unconstitutional by the Supreme Court and then passed again as the Railroad Retirement and Carriers' Taxing Acts of 1935 and 1937, laid the groundwork for a national retirement program for railroad employees that still exists today. In fiscal year 2011, the RRB paid out approximately $10.9 billion in retirement-survivor benefits to roughly 578,000 people.

As part of your predictable retirement income, over time, you will want to be aware of approximately how much in Social Security or Railroad Retirement benefits you can expect to receive once the time comes for you to collect. SSA.gov and RRB.gov can be good resources when researching eligibility requirements for the programs as well as for estimating future retirement benefits payments. Benefits from these federal retirement programs are unique to each individual, and therefore, it is more useful for you to calculate estimates of your own benefit amount to plug into your retirement income plan once the plan has been formulated. In the meantime, I would like to provide you with a few things to keep in mind when thinking about the role Social Security or Railroad Retirement benefits will play in your retirement.

When thinking through government-provided old-age benefits such as Social Security or the Railroad Retirement system, the first question you should ask yourself when planning for retirement is whether you believe the benefits will still exist when it comes time for you to collect. OASDI's woes are well-documented and publicized. We all know the program must be restructured if it has any hope of survival over the coming decades. Therefore, the question becomes, do you think Congress will eventually restructure it, or will the program eventually be scrapped? If you think it will not exist when you would be of the age to collect from it, then obviously you would not want to build Social Security benefits into your retirement income plan. The same goes for Railroad Retirement benefits. If you think that program will not be around for you to benefit from, you will not want to build it into your plan.

All the scary statistics in the world about a struggling federal old-age benefits program, or a plethora of statistics about how easily a program can be fixed, mean nothing when the future is ultimately decided by the ability of a legislature to pass legislation. Of course, passing significant legislation over the past few years is not something that comes easily for Congress. The polarization of the major political parties in today's United States makes passing important pieces of legislation a complex and complicated process.

If you believe your federal old-age benefits will be paid out but are not 100% certain, you can choose not to calculate this type of income in your plan. Also, keep in mind that as facts change in the future, so too can your plan. Your plan can ultimately be adjusted at any time to take into account important events from a dynamic and ever-changing financial and political reality.

Next, if you believe your federal old-age benefits will be around but think that the government, as a way of making sure it can fulfill its promises in nominal terms, will resort to reducing the purchasing power of those benefits, you will want to keep this in mind when planning the inflation protection portion of your retirement portfolio. One way in which the government could slowly erode the purchasing power of OASDI over time would be to change the manner in which the inflation adjustment is calculated. For instance, if inflation is running at 5% a year, but the figure used to calculate cost-of-living adjustments for OASDI recipients is 2%, then the purchasing power of the benefits has decreased. If you multiply this effect over many years, and OASDI income is a major portion of your retirement income, the effects on your standard of living could be quite drastic.

Social Security and the Debt Ceiling

One final point worth mentioning about Social Security relates to the United States debt ceiling, which caused much debate in 2011 and will likely be an issue Congress will have to deal with many more times over the years to come. Only when a long-term solution is reached in terms of funding OASDI, or when the issue of repeatedly having to increase the debt ceiling every few years is eliminated, will the subsequently-described uncertainty disappear.

Going forward, as Social Security is projected to pay out more than it takes in, the program will draw down its trust fund. Given that the trust fund invests in U.S. government securities, if at some point in the future the debt ceiling were not raised, it could cause major problems for Social Security. Any default on Treasuries resulting from a failure to raise the debt ceiling would have devastating effects on the Treasury market and would put the Social Security program in a very precarious position.

When the United States is running a federal budget deficit, it relies on issuing debt to fund the difference between revenues and expenditures. Should the debt ceiling be reached, Congress must pass legislation calling for an increase in the debt ceiling. Without this legislation, the Department of the Treasury would not legally be allowed to issue any net new debt (increase its debt). And without the ability to increase the total amount of its debt, drastic cuts would immediately need to go into effect, as the U.S. relies on the ability to increase its debt in order to fund its planned expenditures. Furthermore, the United States would have a major problem involving the maturing debt in the month the debt ceiling is reached. The August 2011 experience with the debt ceiling provides a good example.

A June 28, 2011 letter from Secretary of the Treasury Timothy Geithner to Senator Jim DeMint states:

"In August of this year, for example, more than $500 billion in U.S. Treasury debt will mature. Under normal circumstances, investors who hold Treasuries purchase new Treasury securities when the debt matures, permitting the United States to pay the principal on this maturing debt."

In other words, the U.S. government is reliant on issuing new debt in order to pay off existing debt that is coming due. The letter continues:

"If investors chose not to purchase a sufficient volume of new Treasury securities, the United States would be required to pay the principal on the maturing debt, and not merely the interest, out of available cash. Yet the Treasury would be unable to make these principal payments without the continued confidence of market participants willing to buy new Treasury securities."

With just under $200 billion in revenues in August 2011 and $500 billion in maturing debt, the U.S. government would have been forced to default had the debt ceiling not been raised and investors holding just over 40% of that maturing debt decided not to roll over their investments. You could have cut 100% of the approximately $300 billion in spending scheduled for August 2011, and it still would not have been enough to pay off the creditors. Perhaps you remember just how focused the media and many legislators were on the interest payment obligations of the U.S. Treasury when explaining to the public the story about there being no danger of a Treasury default. The next time the debt ceiling debate resurfaces, keep in mind the very real issue of *maturing* debt.

The effects of a default would have been catastrophic to the world in so many different ways. But for the purposes of this chapter, remember that a default on U.S. government securities would have devastating consequences on the Social Security Trust Fund. Here is why:

What is known as the Social Security Trust Fund is actually two separate funds called the "Old-Age and Survivors Insurance Trust Fund" and the "Disability Insurance Trust Fund." Both funds are managed by the Bureau of Public Debt, a division of the Department of the Treasury. The funds only hold securities issued by the federal government. There are two types of securities in which the funds invest. One is marketable Treasury securities, which are also available to the public, and the other is "special issues," securities only available to the trust funds. At the time this was written, the trust funds only held "special issues."

There are two types of "special issues": short-term certificates of indebtedness and long-term bonds. According to the Social Security Administration's website, the certificates of indebtedness are issued on a daily basis for the additional revenue not required to meet current expenditures. These securities mature on the June 30 following the date of issuance. The special-issue long-term bonds have maturities ranging from 1 to 15 years.

Now that we know how your tax dollars are invested, as it pertains to Social Security, the question then becomes, what happens to the money used to buy these "special issues"? As it currently states under the "Trust Fund FAQs" page at ssa.gov, "Tax income is deposited on a daily basis and is invested in 'special-issue' securities. The cash exchanged for the securities goes into the general fund of the Treasury and is indistinguishable from other cash in the general fund." In other words, the money collected from Social Security taxes, officially known as the Federal Insurance Contributions Act (FICA), is *spent* and replaced with an IOU from the Department of the Treasury.

With this in mind, you should at least think about the effects of a scenario under which the Treasury cannot issue more debt on a net basis or a situation in which the government defaults on Treasury securities. While an investor holding marketable Treasuries could sell them in the secondary market as a debt ceiling deadline approaches, the situation is different for non-marketable "special issues." Given Congress's recent history of waiting until the last minute to pass important legislation, combined with the general widespread belief that an outright U.S. default will never happen, the investor in marketable debt would likely have ample opportunity to offload the securities if need be. Concerning the debt held by the Social Security trust funds, however, because it is non-marketable (cannot be sold to the public), the trust funds rely entirely on the Department of the Treasury to be able to redeem the IOUs the funds hold. Despite the fact that "special issues" are eligible to be redeemed at any time at face value, they can only be redeemed if there is money available to pay them off.

However, if the Treasury cannot issue new debt on a net basis, very difficult choices will have to be made regarding how to pay off Social Security obligations. With OASDI payments set to increase for years to come, as a result of baby boomers reaching the age of eligibility for Social Security benefits, there could come a day in the future when Social Security, combined with the tremendous future liabilities of Medicare and Medicaid, completely overwhelm incoming federal revenues. Under such a scenario, the Treasury might need to borrow more money to pay off those obligations or to pay off things like food stamps or veterans benefits, which could potentially get bumped aside for Social Security, Medicare, and Medicaid.

As long as the U.S. government runs a federal deficit, and the debt ceiling continues to be a point of contention every so often, beneficiaries of federal benefits will continually be faced with the ongoing uncertainty about whether the Treasury will be able to increase its debt on a net basis to pay off federal benefits.

* * * * *

In closing the discussion on Social Security and Railroad Retirement benefits, I would like to address some of the language often used to describe the structure of various federal benefits programs. Yes, some individuals will call Social Security a Ponzi scheme, a pyramid scheme, or any other emotive word one can think of to describe the structure of OASDI. But for the investor planning for retirement, it is more important to learn as much about federal benefits programs as possible, including their structure, how they operate, and their solvency issues, rather than getting caught up in debates about whether they are or are not Ponzi schemes.

With that information in mind, you should then make a determination about how you want to fit the benefits those programs provide into your retirement plan. Regarding federal benefits, when creating your retirement income plan, make the best determination you can with the facts you have about the future potential nominal and inflation-adjusted values of the income you will receive as well as the potential for an outright default. Then, move on to the next of the various types of predictable income, employer-sponsored pensions.

Chapter 2

Defined Benefit Plans

and

Annuities

Defined Benefit Plans

An employer-sponsored pension, also known as a defined benefit plan, is a type of retirement income fewer and fewer people will be able to benefit from over time, as corporations have been steadily moving away from them for years. In the private sector, the percentage of active employee participants in defined benefit plans has declined dramatically since 1980. According to the Employee Benefit Research Institute's *EBRI Databook on Employee Benefits*, "Chapter 4: Participation in Employee Benefit Programs," last updated in March 2011, the percentage of employees from medium and large private-sector establishments (100 or more employees) participating in defined benefit plans was 84% in 1980. By 1988, the number had dropped to 70%, and by 1997, it had dropped to 50%. From 1997 to 2000, the number plunged 14 percentage points to 36% before slowly working its way down to 30% in 2010. In comparison, the total percentage of employees at medium and large private-sector establishments participating in defined benefit plans *or* defined contribution plans declined from 91% in 1985 to 66% in 2010.

Among small private establishments (99 or fewer employees), only 9% of employees participated in defined benefit plans in 2010. This was down from 22% in 1992. When combining both defined benefit and defined contribution plans, however, 35% of employees at small private establishments participated in the plans in 2010.

Public sector employees still largely enjoy the perks of defined benefit plans, as 93% of full-time state and local government employees were participating in such plans in 1987 and 87% were participating in 2010. When looking at the totals for all defined benefit and defined contribution plans, 98% of full-time state and local government employees participated in such plans in 1987, and 94% participated in 2010.

If you are fortunate enough to have the opportunity to receive a payout from an employer-sponsored pension, keep the following things in mind when thinking about what role the pension should play in your retirement income plan:

First, after determining roughly what your payout will be in your first year of retirement, it will be important to find out whether your pension plan has a cost-of-living adjustment or whether it is a fixed sum that will never change over time. This is important, as it will affect the decision-making process when you turn to the inflation-protection portion of your retirement portfolio. If there will be a cost-of-living adjustment, what determines the amount of the adjustment? If you are able to find out the formula used for the adjustment, it will be quite helpful when working through your income plan for retirement.

Second, what is the risk of your pension plan defaulting on its obligations? By default, I mean a reduction in your benefit or an outright default. For private-sector pensions, how much do you want to rely on the protections provided by the Pension Benefit Guaranty Corporation (PBGC)? The PBGC is a federal agency that provides insurance to traditional private-sector defined benefit plans. In the event of a default, the insurance will pay you, up to certain limits, the benefit you were receiving from your pension plan. At the time this was written, the PBGC was responsible for the pensions of 1,476,000 people and provided insurance protection to roughly 44 million people across 29,100 pension plans.

According to the PBGC's website, the agency is financed in four ways. In the agency's own words, those four ways are: "insurance premiums set by Congress and paid by sponsors of defined benefit plans, investment income, assets from pension plans trusteed by PBGC, and recoveries from the companies formerly responsible for the plans."

Also, keep in mind that a bankruptcy filing by your employer does not necessarily mean a default on pension plan obligations. It is possible for a plan sponsor to emerge from bankruptcy without having terminated the pension plan.

Third, for public sector pensions, what is the risk to your pensions if municipalities, states, or the federal government cut back on spending at any point in the future or find it politically difficult to raise taxes sufficient to cover all pension obligations? Are you 100% confident there will never be a reduction in your payouts or an outright default?

Annuities

Having discussed OASDI, Railroad Retirement benefits, and defined benefit plans, I would like to move on to the portion of your predictable income that will come from a variety of decisions you will have to make.

The question of what to do with the money you save throughout your lifetime can be a stressful and scary proposition for many people. Whether you save through a defined contribution plan, such as a 401(k), through an IRA, or through non-retirement accounts, there are a number of decisions you will have to make when deciding how to generate predictable income in retirement. Even if you decide to have your money professionally managed, it is useful to think through the various ways to bring in income before you sit down with your advisor. This should help you feel more comfortable contributing to the discussion and help you clearly articulate what it is you hope to achieve.

The remaining sources of predictable income addressed in Part I are annuities, dividends from equities or equity-like investments, and fixed income products.

An annuity is essentially an insurance product that provides you income. It works in the following way: You make an investment with an annuity provider, and that provider agrees to make payouts to you at some point in the future. While an in-depth investigation into annuities is beyond the scope of this book, I would like to provide a basic outline of various choices you can pursue if an annuity is something you want to include in your retirement plan.

Immediate and Deferred Annuities: An immediate annuity begins making payments soon after your initial investment is made. A deferred annuity, on the other hand, begins making payments at some point in the future. A deferred annuity has two phases: the accumulation phase, the time during which money is invested, and the distribution phase, the time during which money is paid out.

In both the immediate annuity and the deferred annuity, you can choose a fixed or variable return. With the fixed annuity, you are locking in a fixed income stream for the life of the annuity. With a variable annuity, your payment would vary over time based on the performance of the investments underlying the annuity. You might choose a variable annuity if you are concerned about a rising cost of living reducing the purchasing power of your income stream and want to retain the possibility for higher payments in the future. But just because you leave open the possibility for higher future payments does not mean it will happen. It is even possible to lose money with a variable annuity.

In the context of predictable income, annuities with fixed rates of return provide much more certainty about your future income than variable annuities do. And as Chapter 5 illustrates, there are plenty of other ways to seek inflation protection than just from a variable annuity.

Equity-Indexed Annuity: This annuity provides a minimum rate of return with additional upside potential under certain conditions. The equity-indexed annuity is designed to be a hybrid of a fixed annuity and a variable annuity. The return varies more than that of a fixed annuity but less than that of a variable annuity. In terms of the upside potential to the rate of return, equity-indexed annuities will track a particular index and then, based on the terms of the annuity, credit the annuity with a certain percentage of the index's gain.

If an equity-indexed annuity sounds appealing to you, be sure to read all the literature associated with it and make sure you fully understand in what you are investing. Also be sure you understand all the charges associated with the annuity. Equity-indexed annuities are not the easiest investment product to understand, so it is vital to spend plenty of time reading the fine print if you decide to purchase this type of annuity.

Advanced Life Deferred Annuity: An advanced life deferred annuity might be an option worth exploring. It is similar to a typical deferred annuity in that the payments are not received until a later date. With the advanced life deferred annuity, however, your investment in the annuity typically occurs later in life (in your 60s), and the payments to you typically begin many years after that. This type of annuity can be thought of as longevity insurance, a product meant to protect you from running out of money later in retirement. When the time comes to purchase the annuity, you would invest a smaller percentage of your retirement portfolio, leaving enough to live off until the time comes that the advanced life deferred annuity payments kick in. As with any investment, if this is an option you would like to explore, be sure you fully understand the terms of the product, including what happens to the money upon your death.

Regarding all annuities, if you choose to further investigate this type of predictable income, take a very close look at expenses. From mortality and expense risk charges to surrender charges, annuities are notorious for having high expenses. The possibility of finding an annuity with costs you can afford, however, should not be ruled out.

In terms of how to think through whether an annuity is right for you, one starting point might be to take an honest look at your total investable retirement nest egg. The higher the nest egg, the less likely you may feel that you *need* an annuity. The lower the nest egg, the more likely it is you will struggle to bring in enough income to fund your retirement. But even with a relatively low nest egg, when combining Social Security, possibly a defined benefit plan, and any amount of retirement savings, it can be possible to create your own income stream without feeling forced to rely on an annuity. With this in mind, let's move on to a discussion of dividends from equities or equity-like investments.

Chapter 3

Dividends from Equities

or

Equity-Like Investments

Another form of predictable income for your retirement portfolio can come from the stock market. Many public corporations pay regular dividends, which are monetary distributions to shareholders. By purchasing individual stocks, exchange-traded funds (ETFs), open-end mutual funds, closed-end funds, or unit investment trusts (UITs), you can get exposure to dividend-paying stocks that can provide an income stream in retirement. Two other investments to consider for retirement income purposes are master limited partnerships (MLP) and real estate investment trusts (REIT), both of which can be found on exchanges, just like stocks, and can be purchased by anyone with a brokerage account.

Individual Stocks

If you feel sufficiently confident in your investing abilities to purchase the individual stocks of companies paying regular dividends, there are several things to keep in mind when conducting your research. First, if your top priority from your equity investments is to generate income, make sure you do your due diligence on the sustainability of the dividend being paid out by the company whose stock you would like to purchase. When thinking about the sustainability of a dividend, one metric investors like to look at is the company's dividend payout ratio.

The dividend payout ratio is the percentage of earnings paid to shareholders. One way to calculate it is by dividing the annual dividend per share by the annual earnings per share. There are a few places to find this information. Various financial websites will provide it for free. You will notice, however, that the earnings and dividend numbers provided by different websites do not always match. Two additional places to look for earnings and dividend information are a company's SEC filings and a company's website.

A really high dividend payout ratio (really high is a relative term) should at least make you question the ability of that company to raise dividends in the future and possibly even make you question the ability of the company to sustain the current dividend. Keep in mind that even if the company has what you perceive as a sustainable business, if earnings growth slows to a crawl, future dividend increases might be out of the question. The topic of income growth from dividend raises will be further explored in Chapter 5.

Another thing you should look at if you are a dividend-seeking individual stock investor is the history of dividend payments by the company you are considering buying. Does the company have a track record of increasing dividends every year? Has the company cut its dividend in prior recessions or during unfavorable business climates? Does the company have a history of raising dividends during periods of macroeconomic expansion and holding the dividend steady during slowdowns? This is all important information for retirement income planning purposes, and you should do your best to answer these questions if you decide to purchase dividend-paying stocks as part of your retirement portfolio.

Also, keep in mind that sometimes a company with a history of making steady, reliable dividend payments or even with a history of raising dividends on an annual basis can fall on hard times and suddenly cut the dividend. In recent years, the financial sector, the housing industry, and the shipping industry have all been filled with examples of companies cutting or eliminating their dividends.

Even non-financial companies and companies outside the housing and shipping industries cut their dividends in recent years. General Electric and Pfizer, two widely-known and well-established companies with reliable revenue streams and histories of profitability, cut their dividends in 2009. General Electric cut its quarterly dividend from 31 cents per share to 10 cents per share, a 67.74% drop. As of September 2012, the quarterly dividend stood at 17 cents per share and needed to rise over 82% just to get back to its former level of 31 cents per share. General Electric is expected to announce a dividend increase in the fourth quarter of 2012, which will get the company a bit closer to its pre-dividend-cut level. Likewise, in early 2009, Pfizer cut its quarterly dividend from 32 cents per share to 16 cents per share. As of September 2012, the quarterly dividend stood at 22 cents per share and needed to rise by more than 45% to return to its former level of 32 cents per share.

Yet another non-financial, housing, or shipping company cutting its quarterly dividend in 2009 was Dow Chemical. The dividend cut ended Dow Chemical's streak of consistent, never-cut dividends dating back to 1912. The cut took the quarterly payout from 42 cents per share to 15 cents per share. As of September 2012, Dow Chemical's dividend stood at 32 cents per share and still needed to rise by 31.25% to return to its pre-cut level.

One final example of well-known, large companies cutting dividends is the global oil and gas company BP. After the 2010 Gulf of Mexico oil spill, BP eliminated its quarterly dividend of 84 cents per share for two quarters before reinstating it at 42 cents per share. As of September 2012, the dividend stood at 48 cents per share and needed to rise by 75% to return to its former level.

Some investors might view these dividend cuts from major, well-known, large-cap companies as an opportunity. By buying the stocks in anticipation of the dividends eventually being fully restored to prior levels, one would have an opportunity for respectable increases in the yields on cost for the stocks being purchased.

Yield on cost is the annual dividend divided by the average cost basis for the investment. For example, if XYZ stock is currently trading at $50 per share and pays a $2 per share dividend, the current dividend yield is 4%. But if you bought XYZ stock at $40 per share, the current $2 per share dividend gives you a yield on cost of 5%. Therefore, the dividend yield on your investment is actually 5%, even though the current dividend yield of the company's stock is only 4%.

While it may be tempting to purchase the stocks of blue chip companies that cut their dividends over the past few years, keep in mind that there is no guarantee the dividends will ever be fully restored to their prior levels. The fact that so many well-established companies have, for one reason or another, cut their dividends in recent years is something of which everyone should be mindful when deciding how much of a retirement portfolio should be devoted to dividend-paying equities. Never assume it is impossible for a large, well-established company with a long track record of doing business and paying dividends to run into trouble. What the 2007 to 2012 time period taught us is that so many things once thought impossible are in fact possible.

Exchange-Traded Funds

Beyond individual stocks, you may want to explore exchange-traded funds (ETFs) to aid in the quest for retirement income. An ETF is a fund that consists of various securities and is designed to track a particular index, currency, commodity, or basket of commodities in some way. I say "in some way" because in addition to tracking an index or an asset's price, there are funds designed to track inverse price movements as well as funds that track price movements with leverage added to the positions.

One of the features of an ETF that is appealing to many investors is that its price fluctuates throughout the trading day. This is unlike a traditional open-end mutual fund, which prices once a day after the close of business. Therefore, if you enter an order to buy or sell an ETF, you can get a nearly immediate execution on that order at a price you can more reasonably predict (because you see the current offer price just before entering the order). With an open-end mutual fund, you might enter an order to buy or sell shares only to see the underlying securities move several percentage points in an unfavorable direction before the close of business. You are then stuck accepting the price at the close of business versus receiving a price based on where the underlying securities were trading when you entered the order.

While many pundits will argue that to the buy-and-hold investor, the movements over a few hours should not matter, the truth is that a several percentage point move in just a few hours has become much more common in recent years and can cost an investor large sums of money. If the distinction between ETFs and open-end mutual funds just described piqued your interest, consider spending some time learning about the various exchange-traded products available to investors. Perhaps you will find one that suits your retirement investing needs.

Over the past several years, the growth of ETFs has been explosive. Although ETFs as we know them today have been around since State Street Global Advisors launched the SPDR S&P 500 ETF, ticker symbol SPY, in 1993, the number of ETFs began to really take off around 2005.

According to the Investment Company Institute's (ICI) *2012 Investment Company Fact Book*, the number of ETFs grew from 30 in 1999 to 1,134 in 2011, with most of that growth occurring after 2005. In 2005, there were still only 204 ETFs in existence. At the end of 2011, the net assets of the 1,134 ETFs totaled $1.048 trillion. Of those ETFs, 884 were domestic (U.S.) or international equity ETFs, 75 focused on commodities, currencies, or futures, 7 were hybrids of equity and fixed income, and the remaining 168 focused on bonds. Of the $1.048 trillion of net assets held by ETFs at the end of 2011, 71.97% was held in equity ETFs, 10.42% was held in commodities, currencies, or futures ETFs, and 17.58% was held in bond ETFs. The remaining fraction of a percent was held in hybrid ETFs. Through August 2012, the total net assets held in ETFs continued to grow, reaching nearly $1.215 trillion. The number of ETFs also continued to grow in 2012, reaching 1,216 in August, up from 1,083 one year prior.

If you decide that ETFs or stocks are an investment vehicle you would further like to explore for retirement planning purposes, here are several things to keep in mind:

Make sure you are investing in an ETF or stock with adequate liquidity for your asset size. If you plan to hold 10,000 shares of an ETF, you will want to make sure you can enter and exit your position without causing big price swings in the fund. Some ETFs will swallow up 10,000 shares in the blink of an eye without causing any swings in the share price. With other ETFs, it might take quite some time to fill 10,000 shares, and that size of an order could cause large price swings.

Beyond the ability to enter or exit a position, you should consider the costs of entering or exiting a position. In this case, the cost of doing business is not just the commission paid on the order but also the spread between the bid price and the ask price for the security. The bid is the price at which you can sell. The ask is the price at which you can buy. If you are purchasing a security with a 20 cent bid-ask spread, that 20 cent spread between the prices at which you can immediately buy and sell represents a transaction cost.

Ideally, you will want to find very narrow bid-ask spreads, although that is not always possible. The bid-ask spread is not something everyone will concern themselves with. But if you are frequently buying and selling securities with wide spreads, the costs can add up.

Other things I recommend doing when researching ETFs are to look at the tracking error of the fund relative to the index it attempts to follow; understanding the structure of leveraged ETFs and how their designs affect the returns of investors holding these securities over longer periods of time; looking into the effects of contango on ETFs tracking commodities; understanding the tax consequences of various ETFs, whether they are partnerships, grantor trusts, etc.; and learning about any cost basis quirks that may arise due to the manner in which expenses are managed by the fund. Finally, when it comes to both stocks and ETFs, or any other security for that matter, it is important to avoid confusing volume with liquidity. The topic of liquidity will be further addressed in Chapter 7.

Open-End Funds, Closed-End Funds, Unit Investment Trusts

During your search for predictable retirement income, it may be worthwhile to examine open-end funds, closed-end funds, and unit investment trusts (UIT). These investment vehicles offer investors the opportunity to gain exposure to all sorts of different sectors and industries through baskets of securities with varying risk profiles.

Open-end funds, commonly referred to as mutual funds, have no limits to the number of new shares that can be issued. Shares from open-end funds are purchased directly from the fund itself and do not trade on exchanges. The price investors must pay to purchase or sell shares of an open-end fund is the net asset value per share, plus any applicable fees. Net asset value per share is calculated once per day by subtracting the fund's total liabilities from the fund's total assets and dividing the result by the number of shares outstanding.

Closed-end funds are different from the conventional mutual fund (open-end fund) in that they first issue a fixed number of shares through an initial public offering (IPO). Thereafter, the shares are listed for trading on the secondary market. The share price will fluctuate like that of other publicly traded securities, and shares might be purchased or sold at a discount or a premium to their net asset value. Both open-end and closed-end funds are professionally managed.

Unit investment trusts (UITs) are investment companies with characteristics of both the open- and closed-end fund. Like an open-end mutual fund, investors can redeem shares directly with the trust. Like the closed-end fund, there are only a specific number of shares issued. Unlike open- and closed-end mutual funds, UITs are not designed to be actively managed, instead employing a buy-and-hold approach. Upon the termination date, the trust is dissolved. There are two types of UITs, the equity trust and the bond trust. The bond trust is then further divided into the taxable bond trust and the tax-free bond trust.

According to ICI's *2012 Investment Company Fact Book*, 52.3 million U.S. households and 90.4 million individuals owned mutual funds in 2011. Of the $12.968 trillion in total net assets among U.S. investment companies in 2011, $11.6216 trillion or 89.62% belonged to open-end funds. Closed-end funds and UITs held approximately $238.798 billion and $59.665 billion respectively; the remaining assets were held in ETFs.

In terms of the number of funds available to investors, at the end of 2011, there were 7,637 open-end funds, 634 closed-end funds, and 6,022 UITs. Unlike ETFs, the number of these investment products available to investors has not seen explosive growth in recent years. The number of open-end funds peaked in 2001 at 8,305, closed-end funds recently peaked in 2007 at 663, and UITs hit a high of 13,740 back in 1993.

Beyond being able to distinguish between the different types of funds available to investors, it is important to determine in what exactly the fund in which you are interested invests. It is not wise to simply become enamored by the title of an investment vehicle and assume you can get a sense of its investments and risk profile therefrom. At a minimum, spend a bit of time looking through the holdings of the fund or whatever information is made available to investors and prospective investors regarding the holdings of the fund.

Furthermore, when researching the conventional mutual fund, some important terminology of which to be aware includes front-end load, back-end load, no-load, expense ratio, and 12b-1 fees. A front-end load is a sales charge at the time of purchase, whereas a back-end load is a sales charge at the time of sale. No-load indicates neither a front-end nor a back-end load (no sales charges). Expense ratios are fees the fund charges to pay for operational expenses it incurs during a year, and the 12b-1 fee, included in the fund's expense ratio, is the marketing or distribution fee of a mutual fund. At the time this was written, regulators were working on a 2010 SEC proposal to replace the 12b-1 fee. It is also important to note that mutual funds can sometimes have different classes of shares; these are often designated by a letter to distinguish between the classes.

Real Estate Investment Trusts and Master Limited Partnerships

The last stop on our tour of dividends from equities or equity-like investments will briefly explore real estate investment trusts and master limited partnerships, two additional investments to consider adding to your retirement portfolio.

Real estate investment trusts (REITs) are investment vehicles that invest in real estate or real-estate-related assets. There are essentially three types of REITs: equity REITs, mortgage REITs, and hybrid REITs. Equity REITs invest in and own real estate properties. They make money from the rents they collect. Mortgage REITs loan money to developers or owners of real estate and invest in financial products backed by real estate called mortgage-backed securities (MBS). This type of REIT primarily makes its money from the spread between the interest earned on its investments and the cost of borrowing money to finance its loans and purchases of securities. The hybrid REIT is a combination of the equity REIT and the mortgage REIT. A hybrid REIT invests in properties and real-estate-related financial products and might also loan money for mortgages.

While there are mutual funds and ETFs that invest in REITs, an investor can also purchase individual REITs. Finding an actively traded, dividend-paying REIT is not difficult. What may be difficult, however, is finding a cheap, actively traded, dividend-paying REIT. Some of the most popular REITs performed amazingly well from the March 2009 lows through the summer of 2012. It would not be unreasonable to at least question whether some of the best performing REITs are cheap enough from a valuation perspective for investors in or near retirement. At the end of the day, whether you are interested in REITs that invest in shopping malls, office buildings, apartments, hotels, or MBS, there are plenty of REITs from which to choose.

If you need help generating a list of REITs to research, keep this trick in mind: Find the ticker symbol for an ETF that invests in REITs, go to the ETF's page on its sponsor's website, and search for a list of the ETF's underlying holdings. If an ETF invests in REITs, and you can find a list of that ETF's holdings, you will have plenty of REITs to research further.

This same trick can also be used any other time you are trying to quickly generate a list of companies for a particular sector or industry. Find an ETF designed to track the performance of companies in a specific sector or industry, go to the ETF's page on its sponsor's website, and search for the fund's holdings. In addition to equities, this method can also be used for building lists of individual bonds.

To get started with a list of REITs, spend some time on the websites of the iShares Dow Jones U.S. Real Estate Index Fund, ticker symbol IYR, and the Vanguard REIT ETF, ticker symbol VNQ. After seeing how many REITs these funds hold, you might even decide that it suits you best to purchase a fund instead of trying to pick the perfect REIT yourself.

In terms of the taxation of income from REITs, it is important to note that distributions to investors are typically taxed as ordinary income. If a dividend is considered non-qualified and taxed at ordinary income tax rates, it will not be subject to the preferential tax treatment that qualified dividends are known for. Of course, tax laws may change in the future, affecting both the taxation of REITs and other investments.

When thinking about the risks of investing in REITs, there are, as with most investments, many to keep in mind. There is the risk a REIT might not be sufficiently diversified, not only in terms of property exposure, but also in terms of geographic location exposure. There is interest rate risk in that rising rates would cause higher costs of capital. The use of leverage is another risk investors should consider. There is also the risk of mortgages being worth more than the value of the properties. Therefore, if a mortgage REIT is forced to foreclose on a property, it may recover less than what is owed to it once the property is sold.

Master limited partnerships (MLPs) are investment vehicles that have the tax structure of a limited partnership and investment units that trade on an exchange. Essentially, MLPs are publicly traded partnerships. There are some MLPs, however, that are limited liability companies (LLC) but have chosen the partnership tax structure. Especially for investors with an interest in the energy sector, but also for those with an interest in natural resources and real estate, MLPs are an investment option worth considering. In the low-interest-rate environment of recent years, MLPs have certainly been a place some investors have looked to for yield.

Before investing in MLPs, it is important to spend some time understanding their tax structure. Instead of paying corporate income taxes, the tax liability of an MLP is passed through to the investors (limited partners). This means you are responsible for paying taxes on your proportionate share of the partnership's net income.

From a tax perspective, the MLP's cash distributions are treated differently than its net income. Cash distributions are largely, but not entirely, considered a return of capital and are therefore not immediately taxable. With a return of capital, an investor reduces the cost basis of the original investment until it reaches zero. At that point, any additional cash distributions received are taxable. For example, if your cost basis is $35, and you receive $2 as a return of capital, you would not pay taxes on the return of capital. You would instead reduce your cost basis to $33. Also, if you ever sell your units, you will pay capital gains taxes on the difference between the price at which you sold and the cost basis of your investment.

It is important to fully understand the ramifications of someday selling an asset that has seen a steady reduction in cost basis over time and the major tax liability this could cause you at some point in the future. Instead of paying taxes a little at a time over the years, you will be hit with one large tax bill at the time of sale. Even if you find this acceptable, keep it in mind so you are not shocked by the tax bill when it is time to pay.

Also, due to their partnership structure, MLPs are known for issuing a tax document called a Schedule K-1. It should be noted, however, that exchange-traded products with MLPs as the underlying investments do not necessarily do so. The Alerian MLP Exchange Traded Fund, ticker symbol AMLP, is one example. Another example is the JPMorgan Alerian MLP Index ETN, ticker symbol AMJ.

As a brief aside, exchange-traded notes, or ETNs, should not be confused with exchange-traded funds, or ETFs. Exchange-traded notes are debt products backed by the issuer that attempt to track the returns of some designated benchmark. If the issuer of an ETN declares bankruptcy, you will be waiting in line with the rest of the creditors to recover a portion of your investment. This is markedly different from the structure of ETFs. In the case of an ETF, if the provider of that fund declared bankruptcy, the fund's board of directors could simply decide to hire another provider. The board might also decide to liquidate the fund at the current net asset value.

One final note on taxes and MLPs: If you are considering owning MLPs in a tax-advantaged account, such as an IRA, you should spend some time researching or asking a tax professional about "unrelated business taxable income (UBTI)."

* * * * *

To close out the discussion on purchasing the various assets mentioned in this chapter, it should be noted that many of them require a brokerage account in order to be purchased. Before opening a brokerage account with a financial firm, you will need to spend some time researching not just the quality of the firm itself, but also things such as the commission schedule, potential low balance fees, whether you want a cash account or a margin account, investor research capabilities such as access to analyst reports and charting technology, the ease of navigating through the company's website, and the quality of customer service.

Once you open the brokerage account but before entering your first order, it will be important to learn about the different types of orders available to investors. Learn the difference between a market order and a limit order. Come to understand what a stop loss order is and the different types of stop loss orders that can be entered. If the firm offers contingent orders, learn about those as well. To ensure you execute your retirement plan in the best manner possible, learn as much as you can before jumping in with both feet.

Chapter 4

Fixed Income Products

When it comes to finding predictable income, fixed income products are where many investors end up looking. Fixed income encompasses a wide variety of investments from U.S. Treasury bills, notes, and bonds to corporate and municipal bonds. Owning agency securities, Treasury Inflation-Protected Securities (TIPS), and preferred stocks are three other ways of securing fixed income. Certificates of deposit (CDs) are also a well-known investment product that can provide investors with predictable income. A less distinguished fixed income product among everyday investors is the mortgage-backed security (MBS). Perhaps you are wondering about zero-coupon bonds and convertible bonds. These types of securities are discussed in Part II of this book.

U.S. Treasury Bills, Notes, and Bonds

Treasury bills (T-bill) are government issued securities with maturities of up to 52 weeks. Rather than make formal interest payments, these securities are issued at a discount from their face value and then mature at the face value. For example, perhaps you want to park money in T-bills with a face value of $10,000. Those bills might cost you $9,995 to purchase. When they mature, they will pay you the face value amount of $10,000. The $5 difference between the face value and your purchase price is considered interest income. Depending on whether you purchase bills directly from the Treasury Department or through a broker, there may be different minimum purchase requirements.

Treasury notes are government securities issued in terms ranging from two to ten years. They pay a fixed interest rate semiannually until maturity. Treasury bonds are issued with 30 years to maturity and also pay a fixed interest rate semiannually until maturity. Depending on whether you purchase notes and bonds directly from the Treasury Department or through a broker, there may be different minimum purchase requirements.

What if you want to purchase a Treasury bond with a term-to-maturity of roughly 20 years? Although the U.S. government does not currently issue bonds with 20 years to maturity, you can still purchase one. To do so, you would need to find a bond formerly issued with 30 years to maturity that is now 10 years old. That bond would have 20 years left until maturity. Similarly, if you want to buy a Treasury note with 4 years to maturity, you can, although not as a new issue. This is because the U.S. government does not currently issue a 4-year note. Instead, new issue notes come with maturities of 2, 3, 5, 7, and 10 years. Therefore, in order to purchase a 4-year note, you would need to find a Treasury security originally issued with a longer term-to-maturity that now has only 4 years remaining.

If you want to purchase Treasury securities, you can do so through your broker or you can buy them directly from the Department of the Treasury. The Treasury Department's Bureau of Public Debt manages TreasuryDirect (treasurydirect.gov), a service that allows people to buy and redeem securities directly from the Department of the Treasury rather than going through a third party. Using TreasuryDirect, an investor can purchase bills, notes, bonds, savings bonds, and Treasury Inflation-Protected Securities (TIPS). Not only is TreasuryDirect an option for individual investors, but if you are managing money for clients, you can invest that money through TreasuryDirect as well. If TreasuryDirect is a route you choose to take, be sure to spend some time understanding how it is that TreasuryDirect deals with securities owned by a decedent.

Should you wish to purchase Treasury bills, notes, bonds, or TIPS at an auction, you would do so by entering one of two types of bids: competitive or noncompetitive. In a competitive bid for Treasury bills, you specify the discount rate you are willing to accept. Your bid can be accepted in full, partially accepted, or rejected. When placing a competitive bid for a note, bond, or TIPS, you specify the yield you are willing to accept. Likewise, your bid can be accepted in full, partially accepted, or rejected. Competitive bids are *not* currently accepted by TreasuryDirect. TreasuryDirect does, however, accept noncompetitive bids. With a noncompetitive bid, you agree to accept the yield or the discount rate determined at the auction. By entering a noncompetitive bid, you are guaranteed to receive the full amount of the bills, notes, bonds, or TIPS you requested.

In order to sell marketable Treasury securities held through TreasuryDirect, you must first transfer them to a broker. Keep this in mind if you decide to purchase Treasury products through TreasuryDirect rather than through a broker. But if you are willing to hold a security to maturity, you do not need to transfer it to a broker to receive your funds. TreasuryDirect will deposit the funds into an account of your choosing. For certain securities, you also have the option to reinvest the funds.

Before moving on to a description of the next type of fixed income product, I would like to note something about U.S. Treasury securities that receives very little attention in the financial press. Treasury securities are exempt from state and local income taxes. Therefore, for a more realistic comparison to fully taxable fixed income products, it is necessary to calculate the *taxable-equivalent yield* (TEY) on the Treasuries in which you are considering investing. Calculating the taxable-equivalent yield of a bond is what investors are known to do with municipal bonds.

To calculate the TEY on a Treasury, take the yield being offered in the market and divide it by the difference of one and the sum of the state and local tax rates to which you are subject. For example, if a Treasury you are interested in purchasing is currently offering a 3% yield, and you are subject to 6% in state and local income taxes, the computation would look like this:

3% / (1 − 0.06) = 3.19%.

Therefore, in order to match the yield of a 3% Treasury, you would need to find a security paying interest income subject to federal, state, and local income taxes with a 3.19% yield.

Corporate bonds are debt securities issued by corporations. They come in various shapes and sizes, so to speak, and are often referred to as notes. Secured bonds, unsubordinated unsecured (senior) bonds, and subordinated unsecured (junior) bonds are perhaps the three best known types of corporate bonds. All three rank senior to the preferred stock and common stock of a corporation. With that said, a recent example of a company's attempting to circumvent the normal hierarchy of a corporation's capital structure was certainly an eye-opener for individual bond investors.

In 2011, a bankruptcy of a subsidiary of the company Dynegy seemed to turn the world of investing upside down. Essentially, rather than the parent company's filing for bankruptcy, Dynegy was reorganized in a way that left some of its best assets with shareholders in an attempt to protect shareholders at the expense of bondholders. After the reorganization, Dynegy Holdings, a subsidiary, filed for bankruptcy, leaving bondholders lower on the totem pole than shareholders. In the investing world, that is not supposed to happen since bondholders rank senior to shareholders.

In the end, bondholders sued Dynegy and won, leaving shareholders with just 1% of the company. One of the takeaways from Dynegy's situation is that an investor interested in purchasing individual corporate bonds should not overlook the distinction between debt issued by the parent company and debt issued by a subsidiary. For example, if you were considering investing in a Merrill Lynch or Countrywide Financial corporate bond under the assumption that the parent company, Bank of America, will see the obligations through to maturity, think about the possibility of a spinoff at some point in the future and what that might do to the bonds of the subsidiaries. Two other examples would be the distinction between a Ford Motor Credit Company bond and a Ford Motor Company bond, and the difference between a General Electric Capital Corporation bond and a General Electric Bond. Sometimes the bonds of subsidiaries will even have higher credit ratings than those of the parent company. Does that make you sufficiently comfortable to ignore the possibility of a spinoff's eventually leading to the subsidiary's filing for bankruptcy?

If you are interested in purchasing individual bonds, you will need to know the CUSIP of the bond in order to find it on your broker's trading platform or to have someone else place the order for you (your financial advisor or customer service representative from your broker). CUSIP stands for Committee on Uniform Securities Identification Procedures. It consists of nine characters that include both numbers and letters. You may be surprised to learn that stocks also have CUSIPs. But in the world of equities, investors use ticker symbols to trade stocks. For example, Apple's ticker symbol is AAPL, and Google's is GOOG. In the world of bonds, investors can think of the CUSIP in the same way equity investors think of a stock's ticker symbol. It is what you need to know in order to identify the security you wish to purchase or sell.

Municipal Bonds

Municipal bonds, also known as munis, are debt securities issued by states, cities, counties, or public agencies below the state level (non-federal). These types of bonds are perhaps best known for their federal tax exemption. In general, investors do not pay federal taxes on the interest payments from municipal bonds. Additionally, it is possible to avoid federal, state, and local income taxes when purchasing municipal bonds from the state in which you reside. Of course, within the complex system that is the federal tax code, there are exceptions, and municipal bonds are not exempt from having exceptions.

Furthermore, although a detailed discussion of the alternative minimum tax (AMT) is outside the scope of this book, municipal bond investors should be aware that the tax-exempt status of municipal bond interest does not always extend to the AMT. If you would like to spend some time researching the type of municipal bond interest that is not exempt from federal taxation, start by looking up the term "private activity bond interest."

With respect to municipal bonds being exempt from taxation, it is also important to note that the exemption does not extend to any capital gains realized from selling a municipal bond. In other words, if you buy a bond at 100 cents on the dollar and sell it at 101, realizing a capital gain of 1 cent on the dollar, that capital gain will be subject to federal taxation.

There are two types of municipal bonds: general obligation bonds and revenue bonds. General obligation bonds are bonds backed by the "full faith and credit" of the issuer. Investors would expect the issuer to use its taxing authority to ensure the terms of the bonds are met. This includes the use of sales taxes, income taxes, property taxes, or any other tax it has at its disposal.

Revenue bonds, on the other hand, are not backed by the taxing authority of an issuer but are instead backed by the revenues of a specific project: the project for which the bonds were issued. One such example might be a toll road. Another might be the funding of a public university. Since the project to which the bond is tied does not have taxing authority, and the municipality to which the project is tied is not obligated to pay off the bond, revenue bonds are generally considered riskier than general obligation bonds.

If you are interested in purchasing individual municipal bonds, you should be aware that the secondary market for munis is known to be fairly illiquid, especially for investors trading smaller numbers of bonds. On the whole, municipal bond investors are more of the buy-and-hold type than investors in other well-known parts of the fixed income world. If you decide to purchase an individual municipal bond, it would be wise to do so with the *intent* to hold the bond to maturity. It does not mean you must hold the bond to maturity. But by having the intent to do so from the outset, you will help to frame your expectations for the position and get yourself in a mindset that may help you avoid selling at the wrong time. Furthermore, as part of your due diligence in researching a municipal bond you are interested in purchasing, consider visiting the Municipal Securities Rulemaking Board's website for its "Electronic Municipal Market Access" research center.

Should funds be the way you would prefer to invest in municipal bonds, you will likely be overwhelmed by the large number of choices available to you. Whether you prefer exchange-traded products or traditional mutual funds, there are plenty of funds from which to choose. On the exchange-traded side, here are four funds, each from a different sponsor, to research further: iShares S&P National AMT-Free Municipal Bond Fund, ticker symbol MUB; Van Eck Global Market Vectors High-Yield Municipal Index ETF, ticker symbol HYD; State

Street Global Advisors SPDR Nuveen Barclays Capital Municipal Bond ETF, ticker symbol TFI; and Invesco PowerShares Insured National Municipal Bond Portfolio, ticker symbol PZA.

Regarding traditional mutual funds, you should spend some time on your asset manager's website researching which funds are being offered to clients. Just because you are, for instance, a Fidelity client does not mean you cannot purchase the funds of other companies. In the meantime, here are three municipal bond funds to research further: Vanguard Intermediate-Term Tax-Exempt Fund Investor Shares, ticker symbol VWITX; Fidelity Tax-Free Bond Fund, ticker symbol FTABX; and Wells Fargo Advantage Municipal Bond Fund, Investor Class, ticker symbol SXFIX.

To conclude this discussion of municipal bonds, I will share a few words about calculating the taxable-equivalent yield of a municipal bond. If you have ever used a taxable-equivalent yield calculator on the internet or looked at a formula for calculating taxable-equivalent yield, you are likely to have come across a calculation that took your federal tax *bracket* into account rather than your federal tax *rate*. Many financial websites may suggest they are using your tax rate, but, more often than not, they only offer a drop-down list that includes federal tax brackets as the choices. But make no mistake, just because you are in, say, a 25% federal tax bracket does not mean your tax rate is 25%. It also does not mean you should use 25% as your tax rate when calculating a taxable-equivalent yield for a federally tax-exempt bond you wish to purchase. To better illustrate this point, let's look at an example:

If your taxable income was $100,000 in 2012, and you filed your taxes as "married filing jointly," you fell into the 25% federal tax bracket. Had you purchased a municipal bond yielding 3.00% in 2012, does this mean your taxable-equivalent yield for the bond was 4.00%? According to the taxable-equivalent yield calculators you are likely to find on the internet, the answer is yes. Virtually all those calculators would take the 3.00% federally tax-exempt yield and divide it by 0.75. The 0.75 comes from subtracting your tax "rate" from one. The problem is that most of the calculators assume your tax rate is equal to your tax bracket, which it is not.

If your taxable income was $100,000 in 2012, and none of that income was subject to the preferential tax rate of 15% on dividends or long-term capital gains, then your tax due was $17,060 or 17.06% of your taxable income. Here is how I arrived at $17,060 from $100,000 in taxable income on a "married filing jointly" federal tax return for 2012:

For filers in the 2012 "married filing jointly" 25% tax bracket, the tax due is equal to $9,735 plus 25% of the amount over $70,700. Despite being in the 25% tax bracket, you only get taxed 25% on your taxable income over $70,700, not on your entire income. This is where the taxable-equivalent yield calculators you are likely to stumble upon go wrong. To calculate your actual tax rate, first subtract $70,700 from $100,000 and multiply the difference by 0.25. Then, add this amount, $7,325, to the $9,735 you pay for being in the 25% tax bracket. The sum, $17,060, is the amount of taxes owed. Finally, take this amount and divide it by your total income to find your actual tax rate.

$100,000 − $70,700 = $29,300 × 0.25 = $7,325.

$7,325 + $9,735 = $17,060.

$17,060 / $100,000 = .1706 or 17.06%

So, 17.06% is your actual tax rate on your taxable income of $100,000, not 25%. Additionally, the $17,060 is likely to be an even lower percentage of your gross income since your taxable income is typically lower than your gross income. At the end of the day, do not use your federal income tax bracket as an input in the taxable-equivalent yield calculation for municipal bonds. If you do, the result will be a taxable-equivalent yield that is higher than what you are actually receiving. Instead, use your average tax rate. Also, remember that your average tax rate is likely to change from year to year.

Moreover, be very wary of taxable-equivalent yield calculators you find on the internet, even those offered by major, well-respected financial institutions. Perhaps after this book is published, someone in the industry will get the ball rolling and fix the calculators. An easy fix would be to allow investors to input their own tax rates (which a few calculators do allow) rather than having to choose from a pre-populated drop-down list. But for now, if a taxable-equivalent yield calculator makes you choose a tax bracket (even if it is called a "tax rate") rather than allow you to enter your own number, keep in mind that the calculation you will receive will likely be wrong.

Agency Securities

Agency securities are issued by U.S. government agencies or by government sponsored enterprises (GSEs). Bonds issued by U.S. government agencies, such as the Small Business Association or the Department of Housing and Urban Development, are backed by the "full faith and credit" of the U.S. government. Bonds issued by GSEs do not have the same "full faith and credit backing." However, while the bonds of GSEs are not explicitly guaranteed by the U.S. government, the financial crisis of 2008 showed us that the implicit backing of these enterprises by the U.S. government was indeed strong.

Examples of GSEs include Fannie Mae, Freddie Mac, Federal Home Loan Banks, and the Federal Farm Credit Banks Funding Corporation, a part of the Farm Credit System. The interest payments from Fannie Mae and Freddie Mac are fully taxable at the federal, state, and local levels, whereas the other two aforementioned GSEs currently enjoy state and local tax exemptions. As with other types of investments, any gains or losses from selling an agency bond prior to maturity are taxed as either short-term or long-term capital gains or losses, depending on the length of time the security was owned.

Treasury Inflation-Protected Securities

Treasury Inflation-Protected Securities, also known as TIPS, are securities issued by the Department of the Treasury that are meant to provide inflation protection for the investor. The principal of an investment in TIPS increases and decreases with inflation and deflation. To provide inflation protection, an investor in TIPS will receive the adjusted principal if the principal is above the face value of the securities at maturity. The principal on a TIPS investment is adjusted based on changes in the Consumer Price Index (CPI).

Additionally, to protect against deflation, when TIPS mature, an investor will receive no less than the face value of the securities. In other words, if you purchase TIPS with a face value of $10,000 at 100 cents on the dollar, you will receive no less than your original $10,000 investment at maturity.

Newly issued TIPS are currently auctioned with 5, 10, and 30 years to maturity. The interest rate is fixed, and interest is paid every six months. But just because the interest rate is fixed does not mean the interest *payments* will be fixed. The fixed rate of interest is applied to the adjusted principal value, which means the semiannual interest payments you receive may vary. The interest payment is calculated by multiplying one-half the interest rate (payment made every six months) by the adjusted principal.

For example, if you receive an interest payment of 1% on a $10,000 investment with an adjusted principal of 101 cents on the dollar, the payment would be $101. The next time around, if the adjusted principal were 103 cents on the dollar, the 1% interest payment on the same $10,000 investment would be $103. Likewise, if the adjusted principal declined to 98 cents on the dollar, the 1% interest payment on the $10,000 investment would fall to $98.

TIPS are subject to federal taxation but exempt from state and local income taxes. One important point regarding the taxation of TIPS is that not only is interest taxable in the year received, but increases in your principal are also taxable, even if the bond has yet to mature. In other words, you could be taxed on "income" you did not receive. If the value of your TIPS principal decreases, you would reduce the amount of taxable interest you received from that security up to the amount of the decreased principal adjustment. If that adjustment exceeds the amount of taxable interest from your TIPS, you would treat the excess as an ordinary income loss.

How you then treat that ordinary loss for tax purposes is a bit more complicated, and you should strongly consider consulting a qualified tax advisor who can help you with your specific situation. For the purposes of this book, I would like to provide information found in Title 26 of the Code of Federal Regulations (CFR). The Legal Information Institute of Cornell University Law School provides free access to various laws in the United States on its website. This includes the United States Code and the Code of Federal Regulations.

Information on the taxation of inflation-indexed debt instruments is found in Title 26 of the Code of Federal Regulations, Chapter I, Subchapter A, Part 1, Section 1.1275-7, section "(f) – Special rules," subsection "(1) Deflation adjustments – (i) Holder," which states:

A deflation adjustment reduces the amount of interest otherwise includible in income by a holder with respect to the debt instrument for the taxable year. For purposes of this paragraph (f)(1)(i), interest includes OID, qualified stated interest, and market discount. If the amount of the deflation adjustment exceeds the interest otherwise includible in income by the holder with respect to the debt instrument for the taxable year, the excess is treated as an ordinary loss by the holder for the taxable year. However, the amount treated as an ordinary loss is limited to the amount by which the holder's total interest inclusions on the debt instrument in prior taxable years exceed the total amount treated by the holder as an ordinary loss on the debt instrument in prior taxable years. If the deflation adjustment exceeds the interest otherwise includible in income by the holder with respect to the debt instrument for the taxable year and the amount treated as an ordinary loss for the taxable year, this excess is carried forward to reduce the amount of interest otherwise includible in income by the holder with respect to the debt instrument for subsequent taxable years.

For those readers intrigued by the potential inflation hedge of a TIPS investment, I would like to offer this thought: When relying on inflation adjustments as a hedge against a rising cost of living, it is important to consider whether the index used to calculate the inflation adjustment on your investment is an index that corresponds well to your cost of living experiences. Put more simply, do you trust the Consumer Price Index to do a good job reflecting a rise in your cost of living on an ongoing basis?

If you do not trust the CPI to do a good job keeping up with your cost of living increases, TIPS might not be the investment you want to rely on for inflation protection. Furthermore, if you have any other type of fixed income subject to increases based on the CPI (Social Security for instance), then owning TIPS could create an overreliance on that index to provide you protection from rising prices.

Perhaps you were wondering why preferred stocks were included in the opening paragraph of this chapter as a type of fixed income product. After all, the name "preferred stocks" has the word "stocks" in it. The word "stocks" typically makes people think of equities rather than fixed income.

Preferred stock is a type of security often thought of as a hybrid security, as it has both equity and debt features. It is therefore not surprising that on a company's capital structure, preferred stock falls between common stock and a company's bonds. It ranks higher than common stock and lower than the bonds. In the event of liquidation, preferred shareholders are subordinate to bondholders in terms of a claim on assets but rank higher than common shareholders. Preferred stock typically comes with a fixed dividend rate, which makes this investment product one many investors look to for predictable fixed income.

Furthermore, preferred shareholders also have a higher claim on dividends than common shareholders do, so a common stock's dividend could be cut to zero while the preferred stock continues paying out. In some instances, a corporation might need to delay a preferred stock dividend payment. In this case, an investor would want to be aware of whether the preferred stock is considered cumulative or non-cumulative. With cumulative preferred stock, a company must pay out all missed dividends to shareholders at the time the company resumes paying dividends. Noncumulative preferreds do not pay out missed dividends. In other words, if a company decides not to pay dividends for a certain amount of time, noncumulative preferred shareholders will not receive the payments they would have otherwise received had the company never stopped paying dividends.

Other noteworthy features of preferred stock are that it is usually callable (like a bond), is sometimes convertible into common stock (called convertible preferred stock), typically has no voting rights (unlike common stock), receives a credit rating (like bonds), has a ticker symbol (like stocks), and can have set maturity dates (like a bond) or no maturity date (called a perpetual preferred). Also, the dividend is almost always a fixed rate as a percentage of the preferred stock's par value. This is known as nonparticipating preferred stock. If the par value is

$25 and the fixed rate is 7%, the preferred will pay $1.75 per year in dividends. On occasion, preferred shareholders are given the opportunity to receive dividends greater than the stated dividend. This type of preferred stock is known as participating preferred.

The par value of a preferred stock is important to know not only to figure out the dividend payment each year, but also for another reason. As an example, if an investor is interested in purchasing a callable preferred with a call price at the par value of $25, purchasing the shares above $25 opens the investor up to potential losses. If the preferred stock is trading at $26, should it be called at $25, the investor will lose $1 per share. This is important to keep in mind when researching preferred stocks.

Based on the previous description, you might be thinking preferred stocks sound more like bonds than stocks. That is a fair point. One feature that makes preferred stocks similar to common stocks, and is a very attractive feature for this type of security, is the taxation of the dividend. Dividends from preferred stock are typically eligible for qualified dividend tax rates, assuming all eligibility requirements for receiving qualified dividends have been met. In some cases, required holding periods may differ from those of common stock. If you are interested in researching this issue further, IRS Publication 550 and IRS Publication 17 might be useful. Of course, please keep in mind that tax laws may change in the future, affecting the taxation of preferred securities.

As I mentioned in the previous paragraph, based on many of the features previously described, preferred stocks seem very similar to bonds. They are, in fact, similar enough that I felt it was appropriate to include them in the fixed income chapter. Before moving on to certificates of deposit (CDs), I would like to share a few thoughts about whether everyday investors should consider investments in preferred stock.

If you are an investor who is comfortable purchasing individual bonds, you might consider focusing on junior (subordinated) bonds rather than preferred stock. If, for instance, you are interested in purchasing the preferred stock of a major global bank, it might be possible to find yields among junior bonds comparable to and sometimes even greater than the preferreds. Do not assume preferred stocks always have higher yields than certain bonds of the same company simply because the preferred stock is further down the capital structure. That is not always the case. If you can find higher yields further up the capital structure, that is something to seriously consider.

What if you do find a higher yield in the bonds of a company that always has preferred stock outstanding? Should you definitely take the higher yield? Not necessarily. Another factor to consider is liquidity. In other words, how easy would it be for you to sell the position, if you so desired, and be able to sell it at a price close to where the market is trading?

It is not unusual for many bonds to be quite illiquid, especially when investors are attempting to trade a smaller number of bonds. Corporate bonds are also known for having wide bid-ask spreads. You will have to decide whether the risk of wide bid-ask spreads and the possibility of very little market depth (more on market depth in Chapter 7) is worth the extra yield. You might discover that losing a few points on the bid-ask is not worth the extra basis points in yield (1 basis point = 1/100 of 1%). Of course, there is no guarantee the preferred stock will have narrower spreads or better liquidity than the bond, but all this is something to keep in mind as you do your due diligence in preparation for a purchase.

Then, for the investor who really is not sure whether your typical preferred stock or a subordinated bond is the way to go, some companies even offer an in between stage, in the form of trust preferred securities. These securities are also hybrids of debt and equity and are issued by companies wishing to enjoy the favorable accounting treatment that comes therewith. One thing to keep in mind if you are interested in purchasing trust preferreds is that the income you receive from this type of security is not eligible for qualified dividend tax rates. This is because trust preferreds are technically considered debt securities that pay interest rather than dividends.

Another tax disadvantage of trust preferreds has to do with the tax implications from a deferral of payments to investors, which is often allowed for a certain period of time. Investors are typically liable for income accrued, but not paid out, by the trust preferred security. For additional information on the taxation of preferred securities, consider contacting a qualified tax professional. Also, as a result of legislation passed in the wake of the 2008/2009 financial crisis eliminating the ability of many banks to count trust preferreds as Tier 1 capital, some banks might decide to call their trust preferreds over the next few years. Indeed, this has already started happening. Keep this in mind if you are considering purchasing a trust preferred trading over par.

If you are interested in investing in preferred stock, one resource available on the internet that may be of assistance is the website QuantumOnline.com, which offers investors the ability to find ticker symbols and details on preferred stocks free of charge. Furthermore, if you are more inclined to favor ETFs over single company preferred stock, there are a variety of ETFs currently available for the preferred stock investor. The iShares S&P U.S. Preferred Stock Index Fund, ticker symbol PFF; the Invesco PowerShares Financial Preferred Portfolio, ticker symbol PGF; and the Invesco PowerShares Preferred Portfolio, ticker symbol PGX, are just a few of the currently available ETFs tracking preferred stocks.

Certificates of Deposit

An investment widely considered to be lower risk is a certificate of deposit (CD). A CD is a type of deposit account made with a bank that can be purchased directly from the bank of your choosing or indirectly through your broker. Brokerage firms offer brokered CDs, which are certificates of deposit issued by banks and then resold by the firms to their clients. Certificates of deposit are known for offering higher interest rates than investors would receive on interest-bearing savings or checking accounts and come with federal deposit insurance up to whatever the applicable limits are during the time you are investing.

When you purchase a CD, you invest a certain amount of money for a fixed time period. The time periods can vary widely from as little as several weeks to more than a decade. In return for depositing your money with the bank using a CD, the bank will pay you interest. The frequency of the interest payment could be monthly, quarterly, semiannually, or even at maturity. Maturity refers to the date on which the CD will be redeemed. On the redemption date, you will not only receive any interest due to you, but your initial deposit *should* also be redeemed. I said "*should* also be redeemed" instead of "*will* also be redeemed" because some bank CDs will automatically renew if the CD owner does not notify the bank not to roll the funds over. In my experience, I have yet to see this provision built into a brokered CD. To be safe, if you are purchasing a CD directly from a bank, make sure you find out whether there are automatic renewal provisions. Also, be sure to find out what interest rate the renewed CD will pay. It could be a rate quite different from your original CD's interest rate.

Other important questions to think about when purchasing a CD include:

1. Is there an early withdrawal fee? When dealing directly with a bank, it is quite common for there to be an early withdrawal fee should you decide to sell your CD prior to maturity.

2. Does your broker offer access to the secondary market for brokered CDs? If so, what are the commissions for buying or selling a brokered CD in the secondary market?

3. Are the interest payments fixed or variable? If the interest payments are variable, when and under what conditions will the interest rate change?

4. Is there a survivor option, sometimes known as a "death put" on the CD? A typical survivor option requires the issuer (the bank) to buy back the CD at par (100 cents on the dollar) should the beneficiary of the estate or the executor of the estate choose to exercise the put. It is also possible to find "death puts" on some bonds.

5. Are there call features on the CD? If so, make sure you are aware of the call schedule, which outlines the dates on which the issuer can call the CD away from you. Also make sure you are aware of the call price. Typically, CDs are callable at par (100 cents on the dollar).

6. Are you purchasing an amount that keeps you under the applicable FDIC insured limits? There is no requirement that you remain under the FDIC's insured limits. But to be reasonably assured of full repayment of your deposit should your bank fail, make sure your deposits (including CDs) at any one bank remain

under the applicable limits. Visit FDIC.gov for more information on deposit insurance.

Perhaps you are wondering whether you should go with a brokered CD or deal directly with a bank when investing your money in certificates of deposit. One advantage of using a brokerage account is that you will have access to many different banks from all over the country, allowing you to easily shop for some of the best rates around. Also, the rates you receive from a brokered CD are likely to be higher than you would receive directly from the bank. This is because brokers are often able to negotiate higher interest rates from banks due to the large number of CDs they purchase. Furthermore, the convenience of being able to hold CDs from multiple banks in one place (at one broker) might be viewed as a benefit by some investors.

In addition, with a brokerage account, you will likely have access to the secondary market for CDs, allowing you the opportunity to purchase CDs that have already been issued. If you decide to purchase CDs on the secondary market, keep in mind that should you purchase a CD trading over par and the bank fails, the FDIC will only repay the face value of the CDs plus any accrued interest. In other words, if you purchase $10,000 face value of CDs at a cost of $10,300 and the bank fails before you have a chance to recoup the $300 premium you paid, you will not receive that additional $300 above the face value from the FDIC. You will receive the $10,000 face value plus any interest owed to you at the time the bank failed.

On the flip side, if you purchase a CD at a discount to par and the bank fails, you will receive from the FDIC the difference between par and the discount at which you purchased the CD. In other words, if you pay $9,900 for $10,000 face value of a brokered CD and the bank fails, the FDIC will pay you $10,000 plus any accrued interest.

One disadvantage of using a brokered CD is that the CD will likely be registered in "street name." This means that although the securities are owned by the brokerage customer (you, the investor), they are registered under the name of a brokerage firm. If this makes you uncomfortable, you can go directly to a bank and purchase a CD. I should note, however, that in today's day and age, if you are interested in using a broker to invest your money, it will be difficult, though not impossible, to avoid the "street name" registration. For better or worse, "street name" registration is now ingrained in the financial system.

Mortgage-Backed Securities

In Chapter 3, I mentioned the possibility of investing in mortgage-backed securities (MBS) via real estate investment trusts (REITs). Mortgage-backed securities are securities backed by collections of mortgages. If you are an investor who would prefer to avoid individual mREITs (mortgage REITs), there are bond funds available that invest in mortgage-backed securities. One such example is the iShares Barclays MBS Bond Fund, an exchange-traded fund with the ticker symbol MBB. This ETF tracks the Barclays U.S. MBS Index, an index that includes securities issued by Ginnie Mae, Fannie Mae, and Freddie Mac that have outstanding face values of at least $250 million. The securities also must be U.S. dollar denominated and have fixed interest rates. The fund has historically made monthly payments to the fund's shareholders.

Now that we are several years beyond the peak of the housing bubble in the United States and interest rates have come down dramatically, perhaps you think this is a great time to invest in mortgage-backed securities. After all, with 30-year mortgage rates falling under 4%, refinancing at lower interest rates should help make homes more affordable for homeowners, thus reducing the danger of defaults. But defaults are not the only risk investors in mortgage-backed securities should worry about.

Beyond the more widely known credit and interest rate risks typically associated with bonds, investors in mortgage-backed securities will want to keep prepayment risk in mind as well. Prepayment risk is essentially an offshoot of interest rate risk and refers to the risk that homeowners will pay off their mortgages early via refinancing. This risk increases when interest rates are low.

When prepayments occur in a low-interest-rate environment, it can be quite challenging to find mortgage-backed securities comparable to that which was prepaid. As a result of the prepayment risk, it is important to remember that cash flows for mortgage-backed securities funds can be quite unpredictable. Just because something is good for a consumer/homeowner does not necessarily mean it is good for the investor. Low mortgage rates and refinancings may help make homes more affordable and keep homeowners in their homes, but from the viewpoint of the mortgage-backed security investor, low interest rates can be a double-edged sword (lower interest rates can help homeowners avoid defaulting on their mortgages, but they also increase prepayment risk).

Besides the ETF previously mentioned, there are also additional funds that provide exposure to mortgage-backed securities. If you are interested in finding the perfect one for you, it would be advisable to visit a variety of ETF or mutual fund providers to browse their inventories of funds. A few such providers include, but are not limited to, iShares, PIMCO, Vanguard, Fidelity, and American Funds.

* * * * *

Now that I have outlined various types of fixed income products you could potentially include in a retirement portfolio, let's review several items worth keeping in mind when thinking about fixed income, beginning with opportunity cost.

Opportunity Cost

Nowadays, fixed income, especially U.S. Treasury securities, seems to be a favorite target of investing pundits. There are constantly people predicting that interest rates are about to go much higher and stating that Treasuries are a terrible investment. The truth of the matter is that nobody knows whether ultra-low (from a historical perspective) Treasury rates will go even lower or march higher.

The same goes for other fixed income investments. Take, for example, an investment grade corporate bond with ten or more years to maturity, yielding 5% on a security you think is a good credit risk. If this is not something you are interested in because you want, say, 8% or more on longer-term bonds, then you will likely end up structuring your retirement portfolio with shorter-dated fixed income securities or perhaps higher weightings to other types of financial instruments. But when thinking through the amount you are willing to accept in terms of yield on a fixed income investment you think is a good credit risk, do not forget to factor in the opportunity cost of not investing today.

Opportunity cost refers to the missed opportunity resulting from making one decision rather than another. In this case, is it worth the cost of missing out on interest of 5% per year to wait for higher yields? Or is it worth the cost of missing out on interest of 5% per year to put the money in something else that might have a lower yield and could go down in price?

In the spring of 2009, long-term Treasuries were yielding over 5% on a taxable equivalent basis (Treasuries are exempt from state and local income taxes). Investors who favored ultra-short term Treasuries yielding close to zero, instead of the higher yielding ones, have missed out on several years of 5% yields while waiting for interest rates to go higher. Even if rates do head higher, because of the opportunity cost of waiting in shorter-dated Treasuries yielding close to zero, investors will need rates to move well above 5% to make up for the more than 15% in missed income thus far. Additionally, every day that yields stay low, there is more missed income to make up.

The prior paragraph was not written to imply that Treasuries are currently a good investment. It was simply meant to illustrate that opportunity cost is something worth taking into account when thinking through income opportunities. While rates that are low from a historical perspective may not seem like a good investment, what if rates stay low for several years to come? The opportunity cost of waiting for rates to rise might end up greater than many ever imagined.

Interest Rate Risk and Credit Risk

If you decide to allocate money to bonds, you will need to decide whether you wish to focus on bond funds, individual bonds, or perhaps a combination of both. Let's examine the merits of investing in bond funds versus individual bonds from the perspective of interest rate risk and credit risk.

A simple way to think about interest rate risk is the potential for your assets to experience negative price movements (relative to your purchase price) as a result of interest rate movements. In general, as interest rates rise, bond prices fall. Therefore, if you purchase an individual bond today and rates rise on that bond, the price of the bond will fall.

For the owner of an individual bond, if you plan to hold the bond to maturity and the issuer of the bond does not default, you will eventually get back 100 cents on the dollar. With a bond fund, however, the situation is different. Despite the fact that the underlying bonds will eventually mature at 100 cents on the dollar, assuming no default by the issuer, the price of the fund might fluctuate in a way in which the investor never gets back his or her initial investment. This is because bond funds usually sell their underlying securities prior to maturity. Therefore, the buy-and-hold bond fund investor *typically* has greater interest rate risk than the purchaser of individual bonds who plans to hold the bonds to maturity. I say "typically" because there are some bond funds, called defined-maturity funds, that are designed to hold their underlying securities to maturity. If the individual bond investor does not plan to hold the bonds to maturity, there is, in the short-term, an amount of interest rate risk comparable to a typical bond fund. Over time, as the individual bond moves closer to maturity, the amount of interest rate risk relative to the bond fund diminishes.

Credit risk refers to the risk of the issuer of a bond not fulfilling the terms of the agreement. For instance, credit risk could refer to the risk of not being repaid your principal either in part or in whole. It could also refer to the issuer missing or deferring interest payments. When it comes to investing in individual bonds, each investor assumes the responsibility of measuring credit risk himself or herself. Unless the investor has the wherewithal to diversify across many different individual bonds, credit risk is likely to be more concentrated than it would be should the same investor put money into a well-diversified bond fund.

For instance, in September 2012, the iShares iBoxx $ Investment Grade Corporate Bond Fund, ticker symbol LQD, held over 1,000 different CUSIPs across many different companies. Remember that bond investors should think of CUSIPs in the same way equity investors think of ticker symbols. In order to purchase an individual bond, you need to know the CUSIP, just as you would need to know a stock's ticker symbol in order to purchase that stock.

Similar to LQD, the iShares iBoxx $ High Yield Corporate Bond Fund, ticker symbol HYG, was diversified across more than 600 different CUSIPs in September 2012. As a final example, the iShares S&P National AMT-Free Municipal Bond Fund, ticker symbol MUB, was invested in over 2,000 CUSIPs in September 2012. How many individual investors are likely to be able to match the diversification both across CUSIPs and across corporations or municipalities of a well-managed bond fund? It would require both a significant amount of capital and a significant amount of time for one individual to manage such a portfolio.

Additional Information on Individual Bonds versus Bond Funds

There are several additional things worth considering when deciding between investing your money in individual bonds or bond funds:

1. When investing in bond funds, you will be charged for the operating expenses of the fund by means of fees such as an expense ratio. Because the fees are taken out of the yield, it is easy to forget they are there. By owning individual bonds, you avoid paying the fees that come along with investing in funds. Therefore, you will not be giving up some of your yield, in the form of fees, to a fund manager.

2. Investing in bond funds can provide a level of liquidity you may not have when investing in individual bonds.

3. Currently, the bond market is open from 8 a.m. to 5 p.m. Eastern time whereas the equity market is open from 9:30 a.m. to 4 p.m. Eastern time. If you invest in individual bonds, you will have the ability to buy and sell them during the nine hours the bond market is open. You will likely not have the same luxury with bond funds. I used the word "likely" in the previous sentence because some brokers do give retail clients access to both pre-market and after-hours trading. Therefore, depending on your broker, if you want to buy or sell an exchange-traded bond fund, you could have up to twelve hours each business day (8 a.m. to 8 p.m. Eastern time) to receive an order execution. Be aware, however, that even if your broker does give you access to pre-

market and after-hours trading, liquidity is usually very thin during these times.

4. Investing in individual bonds brings with it a whole host of new investing terms and tax complexities that investing in bond funds likely will not. Some of those terms include accrued market discount, original issue discount, bond premium amortization, and private activity bond interest. If you purchase individual bonds and do your own taxes, you will likely need to spend some time perusing IRS Publication 550, "Investment Income and Expenses."

5. Diversifying across both individual bonds and bond funds is something not to rule out. Perhaps you have a strong sense of the business for a few companies and want to invest in their bonds, but you are not comfortable building a fixed income portfolio with several individual bonds in it. There are so many possible variations to building your retirement portfolio plan that you need not feel like you must choose one product or the other, even within the same asset class.

Credit Ratings

On a final note, whether you are investing in individual bonds or bond funds, keep the following table handy. It will be useful when sorting through individual bonds you are exploring or when doing research on the holdings of a fund that interests you. It outlines the credit ratings used by two credit rating agencies, Moody's and S&P.

Table 4.1

Moody's	S&P
Aaa	AAA
Aa1	AA+
Aa2	AA
Aa3	AA-
A1	A+
A2	A
A3	A-
Baa1	BBB+
Baa2	BBB
Baa3	BBB-
Ba1	BB+
Ba2	BB
Ba3	BB-
B1	B+
B2	B
B3	B-
Caa1	CCC+
Caa2	CCC
Caa3	CCC-
Ca	CC
C	C

The dividing line for debt considered investment grade versus debt considered non-investment grade, also known as high-yield, speculative-grade, or "junk", is between Baa3/BBB- and Ba1/BB+. If your bond has a credit rating of Baa3/BBB- or higher, it is considered investment grade. Otherwise, it is considered non-investment grade.

As you might expect, the lower the credit rating, the higher the rating agencies view the credit risk of the issuer. But just because the rating agencies assign a certain rating to a company's debt does not mean the bond market will agree with the rating. It is not unusual to find bonds with yields much higher or much lower than you might expect given the credit ratings of those bonds. This is because the bond market often attempts to price in changes to a company's health before the rating agencies react.

For example, if you have a Ba1/BB+ rated bond yielding 6.50%, but most other bonds with similar ratings and maturity profiles are yielding 5.00%, then the bond market is saying the Ba1/BB+ rating is too high. If you have a Baa1/BBB+ rated bond yielding 2.00%, but most other bonds with similar ratings and maturity profiles are yielding 3.00%, then the bond market is sending the message that the Baa1/BBB+ rating is too low.

* * * * *

When searching for investment products providing predictable income to build into your retirement portfolio, fixed income should be at the top of the list. Given the low-interest-rate environment much of the world has faced in recent years, it is probably not unusual to encounter people who think it is crazy to purchase fixed income nowadays. But keep in mind that the yields most often quoted by people attempting to belittle fixed income investing are Treasury yields. Treasuries represent just one part of the fixed income market. If the credit risk and yields of Treasury securities are not to your liking, there are other parts of the fixed income world worth exploring. Not only may some fixed income securities have a balance between the credit risk, interest rate risk, and yields you find attractive, but some fixed income products even have elements of inflation protection you might like as well.

Part II

Protecting Your Nest Egg

Building wealth is only part of the retirement planning battle. Making sure your investment portfolio is able to consistently generate enough income while maintaining its purchasing power is another critical part.

The world is currently undergoing an intense financial battle between two powerful forces: inflation and deflation. Central banks around the world are actively working to reflate an international financial system bogged down by too much debt. Money printing and bailouts have become commonplace in an effort to prevent defaults on massive amounts of debt that would likely cause interconnected financial markets around the world to react quite negatively. Those in power want to avoid a deflationary depression at all costs. But will they succeed? And, if they are able to avoid a deflationary spiral through money printing and bailouts, will the cost of avoiding deflation come in the form of out-of-control inflation? Or perhaps the world simply muddles along for years to come, constantly fluctuating between fears of inflation and fears of deflation.

Each of us will have our own opinion about which side will ultimately win out. Some may lean toward inflation; others may lean toward deflation. A third group of investors might prefer to plan for both. This part of the book is meant to help you generate ideas and gain knowledge about how to protect your nest egg from the pernicious effects of both inflation and deflation.

Chapter 5

Inflation Protection

Inflation protection is an important element to any retirement portfolio. But before we can think about how to add inflation protection to a portfolio, we need to first consider what inflation really represents. For the purposes of this book, I would like to define inflation in a way that is easy for people to understand, regardless of their investment savvy.

While you may have heard descriptions of inflation such as "a decline in purchasing power," "too much money chasing too few goods," or "excessive growth of the money supply," let's keep it very simple: Inflation is a rise in prices for the things we buy. Sometimes those price increases are easy to see, and sometimes they are not. A more obvious example of inflation is the cost of healthcare. That is an impossible-not-to-notice type of increase. A less obvious type of inflation would be the number of ounces in a yogurt container going from eight to six while the price remains the same. That, in effect, is a price increase because your money now buys less food for the same price.

Before looking at the various types of inflation protection available to investors, you should first think through to what extent inflation concerns you and to what extent you think inflation will be a problem. Of course, if you are in your 20s, it is virtually impossible to predict how much inflation you will experience between now and your retirement day. Likewise, even if you are in your 60s, in a globalized, fast-paced world with seemingly never-ending bouts of electronic money printing by central banks and massive deficits run by governments, it is hard to predict how financial markets will react in the years to come. In today's day and age, financial markets seem to play a pivotal role in creating inflation, as rising prices stem from the commodity futures markets and eventually feed their way through to consumer goods and services.

But while the financial markets can be difficult to predict, the fact that inflation seems to stem from movements in the financial markets, rather than from rising wages, creates a type of inflation that is actually easier to control than would otherwise be the case. This is because of the significant amounts of leverage currently used in the financial markets and the fact that, on the whole, the world is under-collateralized. When you involve high amounts of leverage, margin call after margin call should be able to eventually break any price increases that are getting too high for comfort. It is just a matter of whether the exchanges have the will, or are pressured enough, to raise margin requirements by a sufficient amount to get the job done.

Naturally, being *able* to stop inflation is different from having the *will* to stop inflation. This is something investors must certainly keep in mind when thinking through how much inflation is realistic over the coming years. Policy makers may be comfortable with an amount of inflation that causes wage growth to be negative in "real" terms (adjusted for inflation) as long as the following occurs: financial markets remain strong, liquidity is abundant, and sufficient consumer spending can be generated at the high end of the income spectrum from the "wealth effect" created by rising equity prices.

The bottom line is that if inflation stems from financial market movements, there are likely various ways investors can hedge their retirement portfolios from the pernicious effect inflation has on fixed income over time. Certainly, times can change, and investors will always need to be on guard. Perhaps in the future, organic economic growth will take hold, and employees will one day enjoy wage increases that keep up with inflation. Such times would create a completely different investing environment then we have been experiencing in recent years. But, for now, let's focus on hedging an income portfolio against inflation in a world in which the monetary spigots are open, uncertainty reigns supreme, and wages are not growing at an impressive rate.

Accordingly, the question is: How do you ensure that you have sufficient income to maintain the type of lifestyle you hope to have during retirement? This is not an easy question to answer, and many people will have many different opinions about how best to achieve this. It is important to note that each person will have his or her own experience with inflation, and that experience may differ widely from official inflation data such as the Consumer Price Index (CPI). You may find that the CPI overstates or perhaps even understates your personal experience with prices.

As you think through how to make sure that your retirement income stream, in conjunction with whatever principal you have to invest, is sufficient to last throughout your golden years, consider the following investments. Of course, some may disagree with the potential for one or more of these investments to act as adequate inflation hedges. Additionally, everyone has a different financial situation, and some of these investments may not be suitable for your portfolio. My hope is that I have generated a list of ideas from which readers can find at least one item of interest. Let's tackle the following list one at a time.

1. Gold, Silver, Platinum, Copper, and Diamonds

2. Dividend Growth Stocks

3. High-Yield Bonds

4. Commodities, excluding Precious Metals and Copper

5. Companies in Industries from Which You Believe Inflationary Pressures Will Arise; Foreign Companies Declaring Dividends in Their Local Currencies; Companies with a Global Presence

6. Variable/Floating-Rate Bonds; Foreign Currency Denominated Bonds

7. Out-of-the-Money Call Options

8. Foreign Currencies

9. Real Estate

10. Art

Gold, the shiny "barbaric relic" the mainstream media and economists love to hate, is often mentioned as an inflation hedge. Of course, when it comes to gold's acting as an inflation hedge, there are those who work to discredit it. Such individuals will cherry-pick certain dates at which gold was trading very high in dollar terms and use those reference points to "prove" that gold does not work as an inflation hedge. One major problem with thinking about gold as an inflation hedge in the traditional sense is that it is *not* an inflation hedge in the traditional sense.

In a fiat currency monetary system, a system under which the currency is given value because a government declares it to have value, gold becomes a store of value rather than a pure play inflation hedge. If inflation hedges are meant to protect your standard of living in a fiat money system that lasts your lifetime, owning gold as an inflation hedge might not always be the best way to protect your purchasing power. Sometimes it will work, other times it may not. But if your goal is to protect yourself from the fiat money system itself, gold is the asset that deserves to be at the top of your list. In other words, if you are worried that the fiat currency in your country might not outlive you, then gold, as a store of value that has stood the test of time, is something you should strongly consider owning.

How much should you concern yourself with the possibility that the current fiat money system does not outlive you? Let me address that by asking one simple question: Are you able to name a fiat money system still used today as a medium of exchange that has been in use for, say, a few hundred years? Do not confuse the fact that the name of a currency may still exist after a few hundred years. After all, just because a currency is called a dollar does not mean the currency system is structured the same way it was a few hundred years ago. This question pertains to the type of money system under which a country operates. Try to name one fiat money system that has lasted even a few hundred years.

I asked this question to help illustrate that fiat currencies have one thing in common: *collapse.* Fiat currency collapses have a long history of consistency across numerous different countries, kingdoms, and empires. When a currency goes fiat, it eventually goes away. The question is simply when.

Maybe "this time is different." But if you believe in the possibility that the mismanagement of fiat currencies by those in power, a mismanagement that has occurred time and time again throughout monetary history, will one day render today's fiat currencies effectively worthless, it seems prudent to own some gold. Gold has stood the test of time as the ultimate store of value. As is often the case in investing, however, there is a caveat: timing.

Timing matters. Perhaps the current system does eventually collapse, but it does so after you have passed on. If you are not concerned about leaving a monetary legacy to the next generation, and you believe today's fiat system will outlive you, then you have a compelling case for *not* owning gold. But you would still need to consider hedging your portfolio in case the road to fiat currency failure is fraught with high inflation.

Before moving on to a discussion of how investors might own gold, I would like to first touch on silver, platinum, and diamonds as inflation hedges. When thinking of silver in terms of its potential to move in price (in fiat currency terms), think of it as gold on steroids. On any given day, it is not unusual for silver to move multiple percentage points more than gold. This is true in both directions.

Generally, I prefer to approach precious metals as stores of value instead of that which will shield me from relatively stable, general increases in the prices of goods and services. There is, however, a case to be made for silver's possibly acting, in some capacity, as a shield from rising prices. This is because of its wider industrial uses. With that said, because of silver's historical role as money in non-fiat money systems and the tremendous rise in investment demand for the metal in recent years, I think it is safer for silver to play a role as a store of value in a portfolio rather than a role as a hedge against steadily rising consumer prices.

There is a belief held by some that rampant price manipulation, pushing prices lower, occurs in the gold and silver markets. If you share this belief, that is even more reason to own gold and silver as stores of value against a collapse of fiat currencies, rather than as pure inflation hedges against rising consumer prices. If you believe the proper value of gold and silver in fiat currency terms is not being unlocked under the current system because of price manipulation, it should not be unimaginable that the true value remains hidden until the fiat system is on the verge of collapse. But if you own gold and silver purely as stores of value against failing fiat currencies, this should be irrelevant to you.

During the 18th century, King Louis XV of France declared platinum the "only metal fit for a king." Perhaps this is true given platinum's relative scarcity to gold and silver. But given its limited historical role as money, its tight supply and demand fundamentals, and its industrial uses, should you wish to purchase this precious metal, it seems fair to think of it in this way: one-part store of value, one-part inflation hedge, and one-part commodity in short supply.

The one-part store of value stems from platinum's being a precious metal that has been experimented with as money in the past and currently can be purchased in bar and coin forms. Also, it is possible to find depository services available to retail and institutional investors directly through a broker. Fidelity, for example, provides its clients access to FideliTrade, a company that sells a wide array of precious metals products and offers storage services for them.

The one-part inflation hedge refers to the fact that platinum does have quite an impressive and growing resume of industrial uses across a variety of products. From the health care sector, to the technology sector, to the automotive industry, platinum has found a home in many products. This, in combination with its tight supply and demand fundamentals, make it a strong candidate to both add to inflationary pressures in the economy and protect investors against those same pressures. Furthermore, investors can easily gain exposure to the fiat price movements of platinum through various exchange-traded products tracking the metal.

A word of caution is warranted when speaking of platinum's industrial demand and potential inflationary pressures therefrom: Platinum's use in catalytic converters is a major component of overall industrial demand for platinum. Should substitutes such as palladium ever take hold, it could have an adverse effect on platinum prices over the longer term. If you are interested in buying platinum because of its industrial uses but are concerned about palladium sapping platinum demand from catalytic converters over time, you could consider splitting, in some way, the investment you intend to make between platinum and palladium. FideliTrade (previously mentioned) does currently sell palladium bullion products.

Last, the one-part commodity in short supply refers to platinum's potential to provide investors with returns above and beyond a typical inflation hedge should a serious supply and demand imbalance develop. Given the incredible concentration of platinum production worldwide (South Africa and Russia produced 86% of the world's platinum in 2011), any disruption in one of those countries, especially in South Africa, could send platinum prices off to the races. According to the U.S. Geological Survey's (USGS) *Mineral Commodity Summaries 2012*, not only did South Africa produce 72.4% of the world's platinum in 2011, but the country also held 95.5% of the world's reserves of platinum-group metals.

Copper may not seem like a logical asset to group with gold, silver, and platinum as a store of value, but it actually can be, just on a smaller scale. Yes, it is true that copper is not considered a precious metal. And while copper coins have popped up over the centuries, a money system based on copper never caught on. Copper has, however, found its way into modern day coins. And when you look at the smallest denomination of coins, the intrinsic value of some in circulation, based on their metal contents, is close to or even greater than their face values. In the United States, two examples include pennies minted in 1982 or earlier and nickels.

The 1909 to 1982 Lincoln copper pennies, which weigh 3.11 grams, are generally made of 95% copper and 5% zinc. In 1982, the U.S. government made the switch to the modern-day Lincoln penny, which weighs 2.5 grams and is 97.5% zinc and 2.5% copper. Pennies minted in 1982 could be of either metal composition. They can be definitively differentiated by weight. Also, an exception to the 1909 to 1982 copper composition is the 1943 penny, which was made of steel with a zinc coating. In 1943, all available copper was needed for the war effort (WWII). But according to the United States Mint's "What's So Special About the 1943 Copper Penny?" there are actually forty 1943 copper pennies in existence. It is believed they were struck by accident. Furthermore, prior to 1962, there was a small amount of tin included in the composition of the penny.

As previously mentioned, the Lincoln copper penny of 1909 to 1982 is made up of 95% copper. At the time this was written, that penny's melt value was actually 2.51 cents, much more than its 1 cent face value. And the melt value has been higher in recent history. In contrast, the 1982-to-present-day Lincoln penny currently has a melt value of just 0.56 cents, only slightly more than half its face value.

The nickel is an example of a U.S. coin currently in circulation that also has a high melt value relative to its face value. The 1946-to-present-day Jefferson nickel weighs 5.00 grams and is made up of 75% copper and 25% nickel. At the time this was written, the nickel's melt value was 5.36 cents, which is more than its face value. In the recent past, the nickel's melt value was actually close to 7 cents. Naturally, the melt value fluctuates each day as the prices of copper and nickel fluctuate.

How might the copper penny and the nickel act as stores of value? In the event of hyperinflation or a complete collapse of the currency, paper currency would become worthless. There is a case to be made, however, that coins with high copper content would be worth far more than their face value and would become one of several de facto currencies if only because of the ease of using coins as a medium of exchange. Furthermore, people might find it easier to deal with smaller denominations for daily purchases such as food rather than using bullion gold, silver, and platinum coins. Moreover, the 75% copper Jefferson nickel, as well as copper pennies, are so widely circulated that millions of people will likely be able to get their hands on them, further making them an easier medium of exchange than other metals.

It is true that the Lincoln copper penny is harder to come by nowadays. You cannot just walk into a bank and get roll after roll of the copper penny. You can, however, still find a few in rolls of pennies, and it is not uncommon to receive them as change when you make purchases with cash. Regarding the nickel, you can easily walk into a bank and get a roll of nickels, making the nickel perhaps the easiest way to invest in physical copper coins. And there's no downside risk to your investment. After all, you are making an exchange with that bank at face value. If the melt value of the coin plunges, you can always return the coin to the bank and get your money back.

In recent years, there has been talk of changing the composition of the nickel to something with less intrinsic value. If this happens, I would imagine today's 75% copper nickel would become more difficult to find relatively quickly, just as the copper penny did after the penny's composition changed, and just as silver dimes and silver quarters did after their compositions changed.

One final note regarding copper coins is that despite their attractive melt values, you should not even consider melting a U.S. coin. That is illegal. It is also illegal to export the coins for melting. The U.S. government has even put a limit on the number of pennies and nickels travelers may legally carry or ship abroad. Given the illegality of melting coins, if you are interested in using pennies and nickels as stores of value, it is best to save them for a time when their intrinsic value might be realized through a legal medium of exchange, i.e., during hyperinflation. But do not forget that storing them can be a challenge. If you are trying to store a large dollar amount, they will be very heavy and will take up a lot of room.

Next up: diamonds. Diamonds are known as a girl's best friend, and in times of currency collapse, they could be an investor's best friend as well. While I would favor diamonds the least as a store of value when comparing them to gold, silver, platinum, or copper, they do represent something many people own or will own and would be able to convert into whatever new currency were to come about. Of course, there are plenty of other things people own that could act as stores of value, and, at first, I was reluctant to mention diamonds in this book. I did so because in recent years, I have read a decent amount about wealthy individuals purchasing diamonds as investments and as stores of value. And soon, all investors will be able to gain exposure to the price movements of physical diamonds.

During the first quarter of 2012, news reports surfaced that a company called IndexIQ filed an S-1 registration statement with the Securities and Exchange Commission (SEC) to launch the IQ Physical Diamond Trust, the first diamonds ETF. According to the registration statement filed with the SEC, the Trust will hold *physical* diamonds. According to another SEC filing (Form N-1A, filed on August 31, 2012), a company called FactorShares is planning to launch the PureFunds ISE Diamond/Gemstone ETF under the ticker symbol GEMS. This ETF would attempt to track the performance of the ISE Gemstone Index. As stated in the SEC filing, the ISE Gemstone Index "tracks the performance of the largest and most liquid companies involved in the gemstone industry, including companies that produce, explore, and sell gemstones." While this ETF would not provide exposure to physical diamonds, it should help to increase awareness of diamonds as an investing alternative.

If diamonds are coming to an exchange near you, allowing investors easy access to its price movements, it is possible the investment demand created by this and any future diamond ETFs could create upward pressure on the price of diamonds. The upward price pressure resulting from ETFs would be similar to that seen in other commodities such as gold. Furthermore, should diamonds successfully work their way into the institutional and everyday investor lexicons, it is possible that one day they will carry significantly more weight as stores of value than copper or platinum currently do. That may take a while, but it is not out of the realm of possibility. It is hard to imagine diamonds catching gold or silver at any time over the next several decades in terms of their demand as a store of value, but I suppose anything is possible.

Now that I have shared some thoughts about investing in gold, silver, platinum, copper, and diamonds, let's talk about the different ways to actually make those investments.

1. Previously, I mentioned FideliTrade as a business that sells and provides storage services for physical metals (gold, silver, platinum, and even palladium). There are other storage providers as well. Additionally, you have the option of purchasing the physical metal (coins or bars) and having it shipped to you. At that point, you would have to figure out how you want to store it. Concerning copper, I already mentioned the option of saving copper pennies and the 75% copper Jefferson nickel. For diamonds, you could own them through jewelry. In some respects, this kills two birds with one stone as the non-diamond part of the jewelry might be gold, silver, platinum, copper, or palladium. You could also buy diamonds on a standalone basis.

2. Exchange-traded products such as ETFs and ETNs are other ways of gaining exposure to the price movements of gold, silver, platinum, copper, and even palladium. What follows is a list of some of the available exchange-traded products designed to track the price of the *physical* metals previously discussed (not the futures). By no means is this a complete list, and by no means am I

implicitly recommending any of these particular products by including them in this list.

Table 5.1

Name	Underlying Commodity	Ticker Symbol
State Street Global Advisors SPDR Gold Shares	Gold	GLD
iShares Gold Trust	Gold	IAU
iShares Silver Trust	Silver	SLV
ETFS Physical Silver Shares	Silver	SIVR
ETFS Physical Platinum Shares	Platinum	PPLT
ETFS Physical Palladium Shares	Palladium	PALL
ETFS Physical Precious Metals Basket Shares	Gold, Silver, Platinum, Palladium	GLTR
IQ Physical Diamond Trust	Diamonds	To Be Determined

You might notice that an exchange-traded product tracking copper is not listed in the table. At this time, a physical copper fund trading on a United States exchange does not exist. ETF Securities does offer an exchange-traded commodity (ETC) called ETFS Physical Copper, which trades on the London Stock Exchange under the symbol PHCU. It attempts to track the London Metal Exchange (LME) cash settlement copper price minus fees. It should be noted that according to ETF Securities, ETFS Physical Copper is not a fund but rather a debt security. The issuer of that debt security is ETFS Industrial Metal Limited (IML).

Regarding the exchange-traded products listed in the previous table, there is some debate about whether certain funds claiming to hold physical metals actually do. Rather than enter into that debate in this book, I would prefer to say the following: If you are interested in purchasing a fund claiming to be backed by physical metals, you should read the prospectus and decide for yourself whether you think it is. Also, depending on your reasons for purchasing certain metals-backed funds and depending on your time frames, you might not care if the funds are backed by physical metals as they claim to be.

3. Trading futures is yet another way for investors to gain exposure to the price movements of gold, silver, platinum, copper, and palladium. Diamond futures are not currently available. As I mentioned, there is not a physical-backed copper exchange-traded product available on a U.S. exchange. There are, however, exchange-traded products available that track, in some capacity, the futures price of copper. Two examples include the iPath Dow Jones-UBS Copper Subindex Total Return ETN, ticker symbol JJC, and the Invesco PowerShares DB Base Metals Fund (an ETF), ticker symbol DBB. Copper futures have approximately a one-third weighting in the base metals fund. The remaining portion of the fund is split between aluminium (British sp.) and zinc.

4. If exposure to the price movements of physical metals or to futures prices of various metals is not your cup of tea, you might consider investing in the stocks of mining companies. This can be done directly with individual stocks, such as Barrick Gold and Newmont Mining, or through exchange-traded funds. Three such funds are the Van Eck Global Market Vectors Gold Miners ETF, ticker symbol GDX; the Van Eck Global Market Vectors Junior Gold Miners ETF, ticker symbol GDXJ; and the Global Funds Global X Silver Miners ETF, ticker symbol SIL.

As previously mentioned, by no means do the exchange-traded products mentioned represent a complete list, and by no means am I implicitly recommending any of these particular products by mentioning them. The same applies to any stocks mentioned. Only you can decide, by yourself or in concert with your financial advisor, which investments are best for you. Also, keep in mind that exchange-traded products tracking futures contracts or physical precious metals may be subject to taxes in a different manner than many investors are used to. Spend time researching the tax implications of each exchange-traded product in which you are interested. The prospectus is often a great place to start.

On a final note, I would be remiss if I concluded this part of the book without mentioning Franklin D. Roosevelt's "Executive Order 6102 – Requiring Gold Coin, Gold Bullion and Gold Certificates to Be Delivered to the Government." The April 5, 1933 executive order from President Roosevelt prohibited "hoarding" of gold coin, gold bullion, and gold certificates and required all persons to deliver to the Federal Reserve or its member banks gold coin, gold bullion, and gold certificates owned by them. There were, however, a few exceptions, such as allowing any one person to hold up to $100 worth of gold coin and gold certificates as well as an exemption for collectors of "rare and unusual coins."

"Hoarding" was defined in Section 1 of the executive order as "the withdrawal and withholding of gold coin, gold bullion or gold certificates from the recognized and customary channels of trade." "Person" was defined in Section 1 of the executive order as "any individual, partnership, association or corporation." Keep this executive order in mind when you decide whether to invest in stores of value and when you think through how much of your assets to allocate to stores of value. Such an order may or may not happen again in the future. I truly do not know. But one thing it helps to illustrate is that, in the past, desperate times have called for desperate measures, even in the land of the free.

In closing, a store of value is a type of inflation hedge that should protect you from hyperinflation and ensure you carry over wealth to the next monetary system if the current one fails. But there are other investments that can act as inflation hedges, especially during more stable periods of inflation. So let's move on from the apocalyptic feeling the metals and diamonds discussion might have caused and turn our attention to investments that can be viewed as more traditional inflation hedges.

What the following inflation hedges have in common, and what makes them lesser stores of value than gold, silver, platinum, copper, diamonds, and even palladium, is that, for the most part, they can only be converted into fiat currency. The one exception is commodity futures, excluding certain metals. But for most investors, the likelihood of having the desire and the ability to take physical delivery of crude oil, corn, or a whole host of other non-precious-metals commodities is virtually zero. Furthermore, if there were ever a run on physical commodities with investors all trying to take delivery at once, the chances are quite good that the exchanges would declare force majeure and simply pay you out in fiat currency. Therefore, I will include commodity futures in the list of investments that act less as stores of value and more as traditional inflation hedges.

Dividend Growth Stocks

One type of inflation hedge that also generates income (unlike metals and diamonds) is dividend growth stocks. Buying dividend growth stocks as an inflation hedge, a strategy that has been growing in popularity in recent years, certainly deserves a look from all investors. In Chapter 3, I mentioned dividend-paying stocks as a potential source of retirement income. Dividend growth investing takes dividend investing to the next level.

The goal of dividend growth investing is to find companies that currently have respectable dividend yields, histories of increasing their dividends, and a reasonable likelihood of increasing their dividends in the future.

Many dividend growth investors like to focus on companies known as "Dividend Aristocrats" when researching companies in which to make new investments. Standard & Poor's (S&P) even created an index known as the "S&P 500 Dividend Aristocrats Index" to track the performance of large capitalization, "blue chip" companies within the S&P 500 that have increased their dividends every year for at least 25 consecutive years. Some examples of such companies include:

Table 5.2

Company	Ticker Symbol
AT&T	T
The Coca-Cola Company	KO
ExxonMobil	XOM
Johnson & Johnson	JNJ
Kimberly-Clark	KMB
McDonald's	MCD
PepsiCo	PEP
Procter & Gamble	PG
Wal-Mart Stores	WMT
3M	MMM

How exactly is dividend growth investing an inflation hedge? From an income standpoint, it acts as an inflation hedge in the following way: If you can rely on certain companies to increase their dividends on an annual basis, your income from that company will continue to grow without having to invest any additional capital. If you find companies willing and able to continually increase their dividends in excess of the inflation rate, you have certainly found an inflation hedge from an income standpoint.

Let's take a look at Johnson & Johnson's quarterly dividend payments and increases for the past ten years:

Table 5.3

Year	Johnson & Johnson's Quarterly Dividend Increased To	Percent Increase From Previous Dividend
2003	$0.240	17.07%
2004	$0.285	18.75%
2005	$0.330	15.79%
2006	$0.375	13.64%
2007	$0.415	10.67%
2008	$0.460	10.84%
2009	$0.490	6.52%
2010	$0.540	10.20%
2011	$0.570	5.56%
2012	$0.610	7.02%

As you can see, the dividend increases ranged from a low of 5.56% in 2011 to a high of 18.75% in 2004. If you bought shares of J&J at its 2002 closing price of $53.71, your yield on cost was 1.53%. As I mentioned in Chapter 3, yield on cost is calculated by taking the annual dividend and dividing it by your average cost basis. Cost basis refers to the original value of your investment. At the end of 2002, Johnson & Johnson was paying a $0.205 quarterly dividend, or $0.82 per year. If your dividend was $0.82 per year and your cost basis was $53.71, your yield on cost would have been $0.82 divided by $53.71, or 1.53%. That 1.53% yield on cost has since grown to 4.54% as a result of the dividend increases previously outlined.

Next, let's take a look at McDonald's dividend payments and increases for the past ten years. McDonald's currently pays a quarterly dividend, but from 2000 to 2007, McDonald's paid an *annual* dividend. To keep things consistent, in the following table, I divided the annual dividends by four to create "quarterly" dividends:

Table 5.4

Year	McDonald's Quarterly Dividend Increased To	Percent Increase From Previous Dividend
2003	$0.1000	70.21%
2004	$0.1375	37.50%
2005	$0.1675	21.82%
2006	$0.2500	49.25%
2007	$0.3750	50.00%
2008	$0.5000	33.33%
2009	$0.5500	10.00%
2010	$0.6100	10.91%
2011	$0.7000	14.75%
2012	$0.7700	10.00%

Over the past decade, McDonald's has certainly been rewarding shareholders with very generous dividend increases. The smallest increases were 10% in 2009 and 2012, and the largest was a whopping 70.21% in 2003. If you bought shares of McDonald's at its 2002 closing price of $16.08, your yield on cost was 1.46%. At the end of 2002, McDonald's was paying an annual dividend of $0.235. If your dividend was $0.235 per year, and your cost basis was $16.08, your yield on cost would have been $0.235 divided by $16.08, or 1.46%. That 1.46% yield on cost has since grown to an incredible 19.15% as a result of the dividend increases previously outlined. Furthermore, during the first nine months of 2012, the stock traded as high as $102.22, which means an investment at $16.08 would have grown by more than 500%. In other words, McDonald's was a fantastic dividend growth stock for the past decade. The question is, can it continue?

In recent years, the annual dividend increases from Johnson & Johnson and especially McDonald's have certainly been impressive. But remember that when you start with a yield on cost below the rate of inflation, it could take a long time to get your yield above the inflation rate by an amount that begins to offset the years your yield was below it. In other words, just because a company increases its dividend every year does not mean you should ignore the starting point. Yes, it is true that the dividend increases from Johnson & Johnson and McDonald's have, collectively, far outpaced the inflation rate since 2002. But beginning with a 1.53% or 1.46% dividend yield might not be an ideal starting point for all dividend growth investors.

For Johnson & Johnson investors, despite consistent, healthy dividend increases for the past decade, it took a long time to grow the yield on cost to 4.54%. It is likely the dividend yield alone did not keep up with the inflation experiences of many Johnson & Johnson investors who owned the stock since the end of 2002. Based on some people's consumer price experiences, the dividend would have spent many years with a negative real yield. The possibility of negative real yields for a period of time is something you have to weigh when entering a dividend growth position.

By 2006, the McDonald's yield on cost, from a $16.08 cost basis, was already yielding over 6% and continued marching much higher. As the yield on cost kept growing on its way to nearly 20%, investors would have offset the negative real rates from the short time period in which the hypothetical McDonald's investment was yielding less than the inflation rate. To test whether this is true, let's take a look at the income returned to McDonald's investors over the past decade, add it to the $16.08 cost basis (from the previous example), and then compare that total to $16.08 adjusted for inflation, using the Bureau of Labor Statistics' "CPI Inflation Calculator."

I know there are people who do not trust the consumer price figures released by the Department of Labor's Bureau of Labor Statistics. I am also aware that the CPI does not correspond to each person's consumer price experiences over time. I am not challenging either of these beliefs/experiences. When I hear or read about people challenging the Consumer Price Index, however, it is not typically because they believe the CPI overstates inflation. More often than not, complaints regarding the CPI are that it is not high enough, failing to capture the full extent of inflation. Therefore, I assume we can agree that the CPI is not *overstating* the inflation experiences of most individuals. Given this, if the dividend payouts fail to keep up with the CPI, we can be reasonably confident that the payouts did not keep up with inflation. If the dividend payouts did outpace the CPI, then we can each determine whether the dividends outpaced the CPI by an amount sufficient to reflect our individual inflation experiences over time.

From the beginning of 2003 through September 2012, McDonald's returned $14.685 in dividends to shareholders. Add that to the $16.08 cost basis, and you have a position worth $30.765 (not adjusted for any taxes paid on dividends or for unrealized capital gains). According to the "CPI Inflation Calculator," that $16.08 investment would have needed to grow to $20.13 by the end of September 2012 in order to keep up with inflation. Since the beginning of 2003, McDonald's dividends have therefore outpaced inflation, as measured by the CPI.

Turning to Johnson & Johnson, let's test whether its dividend payments followed in McDonald's footsteps over the past decade. From the beginning of 2003 through September 2012, J&J returned $16.245 in dividends to shareholders. Add that to the $53.71 cost basis, and you have a position worth $69.955 (not adjusted for any taxes paid on dividends or for unrealized capital gains). According to the "CPI Inflation Calculator," that $53.71 investment would have needed to grow to $67.25 by the end of September 2012 in order to keep up with inflation. Since the beginning of 2003, Johnson & Johnson's dividends have therefore outpaced inflation, as measured by the CPI. But it was a much closer call than McDonald's shareholders experienced.

In fact, after adjusting for federal taxes, it is a very close call. Depending on the U.S. state in which a shareholder resides, some J&J shareholders would have actually experienced a negative real return on the dividends over the past decade when adjusting for taxes. McDonald's shareholders, on the other hand, regardless of their states of residence, would have experienced a positive real return on the dividends, even after adjusting for federal and state taxes.

Some readers may have a few points of contention regarding the dividend growth assessment previously outlined. Let me try to guess a few: First, one must look at total returns on an investment, not just dividend payouts. Total returns would be cash payouts to investors plus unrealized capital gains. Second, reinvesting dividends back into the company from which they came would change the total payout on the original investment, as reinvested dividends would later have more dividends paid against them. In other words, if your original cost basis is $10,000, and you reinvest $200 of dividends into the position, when it comes time for the next dividend payment, it will be on $10,200. Over time, this would increase the amount of dividends paid out on the original $10,000 investment. Third, cherry-picking certain dates will give you different outcomes when assessing investment returns over time. These are fair points of contention, and I will address each one.

1. I agree that total returns are an essential part of any investment. Unless you can absolutely, without a doubt, strictly live off the income generated by an investment, total returns should be of the utmost importance. It can become easy to forget about this if you buy into the idea that stocks will go higher over some undefined "long-term" period of time. By operating under the assumption that stock market indices and "blue chip" stocks will always go higher over time, you might be induced to purchase a stock at a valuation that will harm your total returns over time.

When it comes to the Johnson & Johnson and McDonald's examples, Johnson & Johnson's total returns were enhanced by a respectable amount when including unrealized capital gains while McDonald's total returns were absolutely something to be admired. With that said, given the importance of generating income in retirement, I wanted to focus on the dividend in order to illustrate both how dividend growth investing works and also to make the point that sometimes the growth of a dividend will not be sufficient for you to stay ahead of inflation and/or meet your investment goals.

2. I must admit that I am not a fan of reinvesting dividends under a dividend reinvestment program. I prefer to take the dividends as cash and then reinvest them as I see fit. This could be in the same company's stock when the price is right, in a different company's stock trading at an attractive valuation, or in any other investment I find appealing. I understand why some investors are attracted to dividend reinvestment programs, but up to this point in my investing career, they have yet to win me over.

In the Johnson & Johnson and McDonald's examples, it is true that reinvesting the dividends would provide a compounding effect on the dividends. Over time, this would change the yield on your original cost, and it could be a blessing or a curse as it relates to the total returns, depending on how the stock behaves while you own it.

3. When discussing investment returns over a period of time, cherry-picking certain dates over others as starting or ending points will certainly produce different results. Investors should always be wary of people attempting to sell investments using data that was cherry-picked to make the investments appear better than they really are. The same can also happen in reverse. Some individuals attempt to scare investors out of certain investments by using data that was cherry-picked to make something appear worse than it really is. From what I have seen over the years, cherry-picking data to suit one's position happens quite a bit.

It is true that having purchased Johnson & Johnson in 1997 for less than $30 per share would dramatically change the yield on cost in an investor's favor compared with the example provided earlier. It is also true that investors purchasing McDonald's in early 2012 at around $100 per share would have quickly suffered capital depreciation on their investments and would have had an initial yield on cost of less than 3%. Even in the interest-rate environment of early 2012, a yield under 3% is certainly nothing to write home about.

Certainly, it would have also been fair for me to have chosen the opening price from McDonald's and Johnson & Johnson's last ex-dividend dates of 2002 as the date from which to pull a cost basis. Ex-dividend refers to the date before which you must own shares of a company in order to receive the next dividend. Under that scenario, the J&J cost basis would have been $60.25, making the yield on cost and total return data worse than under my example. Regarding McDonald's, using the opening price from its last ex-dividend date of 2002 would have created a cost basis of $16.66, thereby also lowering the yield on cost and total return slightly. But it would not have changed the fact that McDonald's was a stellar dividend growth stock from the end of 2002 through September 2012.

So yes, changing the dates used in an example illustrating investment returns will have an impact on the final results. I simply chose what seemed like a straightforward time period (one decade) and then took a look at the data. I did not first take a look at what data would work well for my illustrative purposes and then choose the corresponding dates.

Furthermore, I hope this discussion of the various outcomes achievable from cherry-picking dates on a calendar helps drive home the point that despite what some may say, timing matters. I am not saying you should spend your days trying to perfectly time all your investments. But it is important to recognize that timing matters.

Depending on when you invest your money, there could be a wide range of outcomes. Given that your investment time horizon is *not* forever, you might be unfortunate enough to purchase a dividend growth stock that has had its run and will now be on the road to slower earnings growth and slower dividend growth, thus resulting in *multiple contraction*. Of course, if you invested in any number of stocks more than 30 years ago and still held them today, your yield on cost would likely be downright amazing. But just because profits grew fast enough in the past to allow companies to grow their dividends by huge amounts over time does not mean that will happen in the future.

As an aside, a stock's multiple is the number that is multiplied by the earnings per share in order to derive a stock's price. For example, if a company earns $3 per share, and the multiple is 15, the stock price per share is $45 ($3 per share multiplied by 15). Sometimes, when companies experience slowing earnings growth, or when the economy as a whole is growing slower than expected, a stock's multiple will contract. This is where the term multiple contraction comes from. Multiple contraction occurs when equity investors are no longer willing to pay the premium they once were to own a stock.

Let's return to the discussion of timing. The timing of your initial investment can have a profound impact on your returns going forward.

Today, Johnson & Johnson's dividend yield is approximately 3.50%. From an income-generating perspective, that may be an acceptable entry point for dividend growth investors. But there is much more to picking a dividend growth stock than just looking at the yield. Investors must consider whether the company has the capacity to continue increasing its dividends at attractive rates. Investors must also consider whether the stock price itself is trading at attractive levels from a valuation standpoint. After all, while many investors may hope to live strictly off their income in retirement, the truth is that many will have to draw down their principal at some point.

At any time, you may come across a dividend growth stock that you find quite attractive from an income-generating perspective. But if the stock is overvalued, and you plan to operate under the assumption that your equity investments will be trading at no less than your cost basis when the time comes to make withdrawals, it might be prudent to avoid that stock for the time being. Furthermore, if your retirement portfolio will rely on capital appreciation, whether prior to retirement (to get your assets where they need to be so you can retire) or in retirement (as an inflation hedge), keep in mind that even some of the more popular dividend growth stocks can lag the broader market. While dividend yields can be quite supportive for blue chip dividend aristocrats, earnings growth will still matter to market participants. Dividend aristocrats will not receive exemptions over a multi-year period for declining earnings growth or even a noteworthy slowing of earnings growth. Under those scenarios, stock prices are quite likely to react negatively.

Finally, I would like to offer a few closing thoughts on dividend growth investing:

If you are interested in adopting a dividend growth strategy as part of your retirement portfolio, paying attention to the *payout ratio* (discussed in Chapter 3) is important. High dividend payout ratios may foreshadow slowing dividend growth. What is considered high? A high dividend payout ratio is a relative term. You should not, for instance, compare the payout ratio of a REIT to that of a tech company and immediately conclude that a REIT's payout ratio is too high because tech companies sport much lower payout ratios.

In general, take a look at the payout ratio and make a determination as to whether the company you are researching can afford to continue increasing its dividends at attractive rates given the percentage of profits it already pays out. When attempting to make this determination, think through things such as general trends in that company's sales, the health of the industry as a whole, capital expenditures, interest on debt, and any other thing you think might reduce the amount of cash available for dividend increases in the future.

Also, keep an eye on dividend *tax rates* going forward. During times when tax rates on dividends go up, you should not be surprised to see a bit of multiple contraction in your dividend growth stocks. The same goes for stocks in general during times capital gains taxes go up. It does not mean the stock price cannot go higher. A stock's price can go higher even with multiple contraction, but that requires a company to grow earnings to an extent that the earnings offset the decline in the multiple.

If you are uncomfortable picking individual stocks for a dividend growth strategy, there are exchange-traded products available that you could consider buying instead. State Street Global Advisors SPDR S&P Dividend ETF, ticker symbol SDY, is one example. It aims to track the returns of the S&P High Yield Dividend Aristocrats Index. Another example is the Vanguard Dividend Appreciation ETF, ticker symbol VIG.

With respect to the *dividend aristocrats*, remember that just because a company currently shows up on the list does not mean it will do so forever. While being on the dividend aristocrats list does show a tendency to raise dividends on a yearly basis, it does not *guarantee* a dividend raise on a yearly basis. All the list does is inform investors about the past. It is up to each investor to determine whether the past will repeat itself in the future.

I would like to close the dividend growth discussion by noting that dividend growth investing is a retirement income strategy that has certainly captured my attention over the years. I own certain stocks in my retirement portfolio in large part because of the dividend growth I believe they will provide over time. With that said, while dividend growth investing can act as a decent inflation hedge during times of low-to-moderate inflation, it is no panacea. There are no free lunches in investing, and you should always spend an adequate amount of time researching the potential pitfalls of any investment opportunity. The drawbacks you discover might not change your mind about making a certain investment. But understanding the potential difficulties of any investment you make should help you better assess when it is time to exit, hold steady, or perhaps even buy more.

High-Yield Bonds

Do you find the very mention of the word "bond" in a chapter about inflation hedging confusing? After all, bonds are widely known for providing fixed interest payments and for having limited potential for capital appreciation. Believe it or not, certain bonds can play a role as an inflation hedge for some investors. High-yield bonds are one example.

High-yield bonds, also known as non-investment grade, speculative-grade, or "junk" bonds, are debt securities that have received credit ratings of below investment grade. Bonds with non-investment grade ratings are generally thought to have more credit risk than those with investment grade ratings. In order to compensate investors for that extra credit risk, the market typically offers higher yields on non-investment grade bonds than it does on bonds with higher credit ratings. As a brief review, in Chapter 4, I described credit risk as the risk of the issuer of a bond not fulfilling the terms of the agreement. For example, credit risk could refer to the risk of not being repaid your principal either in part or in whole. It could also refer to the issuer missing or deferring interest payments.

In general, the higher the credit risk of an issuer, the higher the yield on that issuer's bonds. If I am thinking about loaning money to two different companies, and I judge one company to be a greater risk of not paying me back, then in order for me to even consider loaning money to the higher credit risk, I would expect a higher yield on the bond.

High-yield bonds can belong to companies, municipalities, or even countries. You can purchase the individual bonds belonging to a specific issuer or you can purchase a fund with underlying holdings containing non-investment grade ratings. Please refer to the discussion in Chapter 4 for things to think about when deciding whether individual bonds or bond funds are right for you.

How can owning high-yield bonds act as an inflation hedge? To maintain the purchasing power of your money, you will want to realize an after-tax return on your portfolio equal to or in excess of your personal inflation rate. If you believe your personal inflation rate will remain in the 0% to 5% range over an extended period of time, and you can create a diversified high-yield bond portfolio of 7% of higher, there is a very good chance you will be able to maintain the purchasing power of the money invested in high-yield bonds. This works especially well for investors who are building a retirement portfolio but are not yet dependent on that portfolio to cover living expenses.

When you are actually in retirement and depend on your portfolio to generate income for you to live off, things become a bit more complicated. If, in retirement, you are spending all the income your portfolio generates, you will need unrealized capital gains to ensure your principal's purchasing power is maintained. You can still own bonds in such a situation, but in order to maintain the purchasing power of the portfolio, your yearly capital appreciation will likely need to come from other assets. Among all retirees, I suspect there are relatively few who have built up sufficient assets to live strictly off the income. Most investors in retirement are likely to worry less about maintaining the purchasing power of their principal and instead be in a position in which they simply try not to draw down their principal too quickly.

If you are in a position in which your portfolio will need to be drawn down during retirement, your focus should not be on maintaining the purchasing power of your principal but rather on maintaining the purchasing power of your retirement income. In other words, your focus will be on making sure your income increases by enough to offset any increases in your expenses. Drawing down your portfolio can help accomplish this. But before resorting to taking withdrawals from your portfolio, carefully consider all higher-yielding securities available to you. This includes high-yield bonds.

You may have heard that in an inflationary environment, all bond prices are destined to go down. If you are eventually forced to sell your bond investments to pay the bills, and those bonds have declined in value, that would clearly not be an ideal situation. The good news about high-yield bonds, however, is that their prices are not destined to decline in an inflationary environment. Concerning high-yield bonds, once again, timing matters. If you purchase high-yield bonds when spreads to benchmark Treasury yields are wide, then even in an inflationary environment, your high-yield bonds have a good chance of holding up reasonably well. Let me explain using the "BofA Merrill Lynch US High Yield Master II Option-Adjusted Spread."

The aforementioned BofA Merrill Lynch high-yield spread compares to Treasuries an index of U.S. dollar denominated bonds that are rated non-investment grade, have more than one year remaining until maturity, and at least $100 million of debt outstanding. In early summer 2012, the spread to Treasuries was 652 basis points. One basis point equals $1/100^{th}$ of a percent, so 652 basis points equals 6.52%. An easy way to think about this spread is that the high-yield bond market, as a whole, is yielding 652 basis points more than the Treasury market. Different components of the high-yield bond market will have their own individual spreads to Treasuries.

During the 2008/2009 financial crisis, the high-yield spread reached 2,182 basis points. During the bear market in "risk assets" that followed the bursting of the tech bubble, this spread reached 1,120 basis points. Using the high points of each of the last two bear markets, 652 basis points might not seem very attractive. But when times were good for financial markets in the late 1990s and 2004 to early 2007, it was incredibly common to see this spread under 400 basis points and not unusual to see it under 300 basis points. Even in the post-2008/2009 financial crisis world, the spread got as low as the 450 to 500 basis points region for multiple months during the first half of 2011.

In other words, when the financial markets enter a long period of stability, high-yield spreads have shown a tendency to narrow significantly. A narrowing of the spread would provide a hedge against rising benchmark Treasury yields reacting to higher inflation expectations in the economy.

As an example, let's say the 5-year Treasury yield rises to 4% in reaction to an improving economy and higher inflation expectations. As long as the 652 basis points (or 6.52 percentage points above the Treasury yield) spread narrows by an equivalent amount to the rise in Treasury yields, they would offset each other, thereby theoretically creating relatively no change in the price of your portfolio. I use the word "theoretically" because the slope of the yield curve and the duration of your portfolio could slightly change the overall performance of your portfolio in either direction.

Would it be possible for the high-yield spread to narrow to around 250 basis points (2.50 percentage points above Treasuries)? It has been there before, most recently in June 2007. The point is that if you purchase high-yield bonds when spreads are historically wide, there is a very good chance you have hedged yourself against rising benchmark Treasury rates. While a 652 basis points spread does represent value from a historical perspective, it is not the type of level at which I would go all-in. It is, however, a level around which I have scaled into high-yield bond positions.

What if inflation moves beyond the 0% to 5% range? Can high-yield bonds still work under that scenario? It all depends on your timing. If you create a diversified high-yield bond portfolio at a double-digit spread to Treasuries and have the capacity to hold it through whatever economic struggles caused the high-yield market's spread to widen that far, there is a strong likelihood the money you invested in high-yield bonds will be well-positioned for inflation moving into the 5% to 10% range.

Or, if you are completely uninterested in trying to time the high-yield market, you can always follow the same advice financial advisors provide to equity investors: Buy on the dip. Adding to your position on pullbacks in prices does not just work for stocks. It is a compelling strategy for bond investors as well. If you start buying with yields in the 7% range, only to see spreads widen and yields move higher, you can always add to your position, thereby raising the average yield in your portfolio.

When building your retirement portfolio, keep in mind that the high-yield bond market offers opportunities for investors to get above-average yields in excess of many people's overall inflation experiences. Prices on high-yield bonds can vary widely over time, but just as equity investors view bear markets as opportunities to add to positions, so too can investors in high-yield bonds.

Unsurprisingly, should hyperinflation ever rear its ugly head, bonds are not the place you want to invest your money. In the case of hyperinflation, it makes more sense to favor securities that will realize mark-to-market gains, as the chances are quite good most people will have to draw down the principal they invested just to survive.

If building a portfolio of individual non-investment grade bonds is a route you want to explore, when performing your research, your focus should be on bonds with ratings of Ba1/BB+ (Moody's/S&P) and below. The next table outlines the various non-investment grade ratings from Moody's and S&P.

Table 5.5

Moody's	S&P
Ba1	BB+
Ba2	BB
Ba3	BB-
B1	B+
B2	B
B3	B-
Caa1	CCC+
Caa2	CCC
Caa3	CCC-
Ca	CC
C	C

In my personal portfolio, I avoid buying individual bonds with ratings below B3/B-. It is always possible that a bond I own could get downgraded to below B3/B-, but I have yet to initiate positions at those levels. The credit risk associated with bonds that carry ratings below single B is so great that I prefer to gain exposure to that part of the high-yield market through exchange-traded funds.

The next table shows the name and ticker symbol of ten different exchange-traded products focused on high-yield bonds:

Table 5.6

Name	Underlying Focus	Ticker Symbol
iShares iBoxx $ High Yield Corporate Bond Fund	Corporate	HYG
State Street Global Advisors SPDR Barclays Capital High Yield Bond ETF	Corporate	JNK
Invesco PowerShares Fundamental High Yield Corporate Bond Portfolio	Corporate	PHB
AdvisorShares Peritus High Yield ETF	Corporate	HYLD
PIMCO 0-5 Year High Yield Corporate Bond Index Fund	Corporate	HYS
iShares Global High Yield Corporate Bond Fund	Corporate	GHYG
iShares Global ex USD High Yield Corporate Bond Fund	Corporate	HYXU
iShares B – Ca Rated Corporate Bond Fund	Corporate	QLTC
iShares Emerging Markets High Yield Bond Fund	Sovereign (but does have some corporates)	EMHY
Van Eck Global Market Vectors High-Yield Municipal Index ETF	Municipal	HYD

If non-exchange-traded products are more to your liking, a few with high-yield bond exposure are the Fidelity High Income Fund, ticker symbol SPHIX; the Vanguard High-Yield Corporate Fund Investor Shares, ticker symbol VWEHX; and the TIAA-CREF Funds High-Yield Retail Class, ticker symbol TIYRX.

Furthermore, if you are interested in the benefits of a bond maturing at par but prefer not to take on the risk of choosing individual bonds for your portfolio, you might consider researching Guggenheim's BulletShares High Yield Corporate Bond ETFs. These funds are known as defined-maturity exchange-traded funds (ETFs) and are very similar to traditional bond ETFs with one huge exception: Defined maturity ETFs have a specific maturity date. Upon maturity, the ETF distributes the fund's net assets to shareholders and ceases operations.

I am aware that for many investors, the term "junk bonds" might evoke fears of excessive risk and defaults. Perhaps this is the case for you. If so, I would like to challenge those fears by providing some facts on both default rates and recovery rates.

According to Moody's Investors Service's *Annual Default Study: Corporate Default and Recovery Rates, 1920-2011*, the average annual default rate for non-investment grade corporate bonds from 1920 to 2011 was 2.802%. The highest default rate among "junk" bonds in any single year was 15.641% in 1933.

Among corporate bonds with Ba1 to Ba3 ratings, the average annual default rate from 1920 to 2011 was just 1.073%. Corporate bonds with B1 to B3 ratings had average annual default rates of 3.423% during the same time period. For corporates with ratings of Caa1 and below, the average annual default rate from 1920 to 2011 was 13.769%, including 23 years during which the default rate was over 20%.

With respect to recovery rates, remember that as the owner of a bond, you are senior in the capital structure to shareholders. Therefore, in the event of bankruptcy, it is reasonable to expect a much higher recovery rate than that which shareholders of the common stock will receive. According to the same study by Moody's, from 1987 to 2011, the average recovery rate for senior unsecured corporate bonds was 48.5%. This means that if you owned a senior unsecured individual bond, and the issuer defaulted on its debt, you would have recovered, on average, 48.5 cents on the dollar from 1987 to 2011. During the same time period, the average recovery rate for subordinated bonds was 28.7% or 28.7 cents on the dollar.

On a final note, in Chapter 6, you may notice that I left high-yield bonds off the list of deflation protection investments. I do think high-yield bonds can serve as a deflation hedge, but keep in mind that during periods of deflation, highly indebted companies may struggle to meet their obligations. While the yields in the high-yield bond space will certainly be attractive during periods of deflation, you will need to be very selective about the companies to which you want exposure.

Commodities, excluding Precious Metals and Copper

In recent years, commodities seem to have become the go-to place for investors hoping to protect their money from inflation. And with the rapid expansion of exchange-traded products over the past decade, the world of commodities has become much easier for all types of investors to access. Rather than having to trade commodity futures, investors can now express an opinion on any number of commodities by buying ETFs and ETNs that track the performance of those commodities.

In a world in which unconventional monetary policy and massive fiscal deficits are pervasive, investors fearful of too much money chasing too few goods have chosen commodities as an asset class in which to hide. Investors flocking to commodities also like to tell the story about growth in the emerging markets eventually driving commodity prices to untold heights. Perhaps they will someday be right. Perhaps demand from higher growth economies around the world, combined with investors seeking shelter from central bank money printing operations, will create the perfect storm for commodity prices. Your job as an investor is to figure out whether the story behind commodities is one you believe and whether commodity prices, in general, have already priced in those known unknowns.

Before you jump on board the commodities bandwagon in order to protect yourself from inflation, consider these questions:

1. During a balance sheet recession, what are the potential inflationary effects of unconventional monetary policy? A "balance sheet recession" refers to a period of time during which the priorities of the private sector have changed so that minimizing debt is more of a focus than taking on debt. "Unconventional monetary policy" refers to central bank programs that are colloquially referred to as "money printing."

2. Is inflation coming from money in the hands of everyday people chasing too few goods? Or is it coming from too much money chasing too few financial assets. In other words, is inflation coming from investors creating their own realities by chasing returns in highly leveraged commodities markets?

3. To what extent does inflation come from public companies feeling pressure from shareholders to continuously increase profits and then reacting to that pressure by raising prices to offset the producer price inflation created by commodity investors?

4. What would happen to commodity prices if investors did not have the ability to leverage up as much as they currently do? Does a highly leveraged market help investors discover the "true" price of an asset?

5. Is investing in assets that do not produce any income, do not operate as traditional stores of value, and have a history of very large price swings in very short periods of time the right type of traditional inflation hedge for your retirement portfolio?

Please keep in mind that I am not trying to convince you one way or the other about investing in commodities. I am simply offering a series of questions meant to challenge investors to think about where inflation is coming from in today's day and age, whether those pressures are sustainable, and whether the commodity story has largely priced in the known unknowns regarding future supply and demand dynamics. If, after thinking through these various questions, you are still interested in investing in commodities, you will need to decide whether directly trading futures or accessing the futures market via exchange-traded products is the way to go.

If you are leaning toward trading commodity futures yourself, make sure you fully understand the margin requirements associated therewith as well as the effects contango can have on your portfolio over an extended period of time. Margin refers to the amount of money you must put up in order to trade a futures contract. The easiest way to think about contango is a near-month futures contract trading at a lower price than a futures contract further out in time. Therefore, to maintain a constant presence in a futures market in contango, you might be forced to sell one contract at a lower price than you will buy the next contract. Selling low and buying high is not typically thought of as the road to investing success.

Even certain exchange-traded products suffer from the effects of contango. Two popular ETFs that have suffered severely under contango are the United States Natural Gas Fund, ticker symbol UNG, and the United States Oil Fund, ticker symbol USO. Both ETFs track the near-month futures contract for their respective commodities until those contracts are within two weeks of expiration, at which time the funds track the next nearest month. This strategy has been an absolute disaster for these ETFs, especially so for UNG, and help illustrate the effects contango can have on commodity investors. Furthermore, should natural gas or crude oil ever move into backwardation, the opposite type of price performance for these funds should occur as near month contracts are sold for higher prices than where future month contracts are trading. In that case, the ETFs would be selling high and buying low when rolling into new contracts.

If you made it through the series of questions I posed with a continued interest in commodities investing but prefer not to trade futures yourself and do not mind the possibility of contango eating away at potential future profits, the following table may be of interest. It includes the names and ticker symbols for various commodity-related exchange-traded products tracking futures prices (excluding precious metals and copper, with one exception). By no means should this be considered a complete list of all the exchange-traded products tracking commodities. There are a lot.

Table 5.7

Name	Underlying Commodity Futures Tracked	Ticker Symbol
Invesco PowerShares DB Commodity Index Tracking Fund	WTI and Brent Crude Oil, Heating Oil, Gasoline, Natural Gas, Gold, Silver, Aluminium, Zinc, Copper, Corn, Wheat, Soybeans, Sugar	DBC
Invesco PowerShares DB Agriculture Fund	Cattle, Cocoa, Coffee, Corn, Cotton, Lean Hogs, Soybeans, Sugar, Wheat	DBA
United States Oil Fund	WTI Light, Sweet Crude Oil	USO
United States 12 Month Oil Fund	WTI Light, Sweet Crude Oil (12 different contracts)	USL
United States Gasoline Fund	RBOB Gasoline	UGA
United States Diesel-Heating Oil Fund	Heating Oil	UHN
United States Natural Gas Fund	Natural Gas	UNG
United States 12 Month Natural Gas Fund	Natural Gas (12 different contracts)	UNL
iPath Dow Jones-UBS Sugar Subindex Total Return ETN	Sugar	SGG
iPath Dow Jones-UBS Cotton Subindex Total Return ETN	Cotton	BAL
iPath Dow Jones-UBS Coffee Subindex Total Return ETN	Coffee	JO

When doing your research on futures trading or on investing in commodity-focused exchange-traded products, pay particular attention to how taxes are reported for such investments. Specifically, you will want to learn about Schedule K-1, section 1256 contracts, and mark-to-market year-end accounting. If you have any questions regarding the tax implications of investing in commodities, please consult a qualified tax advisor.

Last, as I mentioned earlier in this chapter, if you are investing in commodity futures with the intent of taking delivery at a time when you will want the underlying commodity to serve as a store of value, the chances are good that plenty of other investors will be trying to take delivery at the same time. Under that scenario, you should not be surprised if the exchanges declare force majeure and you end up being paid out in the very fiat currency you were hoping to avoid.

Companies in Industries from Which You Believe Inflationary Pressures Will Arise; Foreign Companies Declaring Dividends in Their Local Currencies; Companies with a Global Presence

Investing in stocks can be a decent inflation hedge during times of low-to-moderate inflation. This is especially true during times when companies have pricing power, allowing them to raise the prices of their goods and services without negatively affecting demand. Earlier in this chapter, I discussed dividend growth investing as a potential inflation hedge. Another target for equity investors looking for inflation protection is to acquire the stocks of companies that operate in industries from which you believe inflationary pressures will arise. Also, investing in the stocks of foreign companies declaring their dividend payments in their local currencies as well as investing in the stocks of companies with a global presence are ways to consider protecting the purchasing power of your investments.

If you believe commodity price pressures will be the driver of inflation, you might consider investing in the stocks of companies that will benefit from rising energy prices or from rising prices for commodities such as soybeans, corn, and wheat. If your biggest inflation worries come from price increases in health care, you might consider investing in the health insurance providers or large capitalization pharmaceutical stocks. But keep in mind that just because your health care costs are going higher over time does not necessarily mean health care stocks will be a good investment going forward. Should picking individual stocks not be your forte, there are likely ETFs or mutual funds available that fit your criteria.

If you like the idea of purchasing the stocks of companies that operate in industries from which you believe inflationary pressures will emerge, it is important to differentiate between companies with pricing power and those without pricing power. For example, although you may see your grocery bills creeping higher each month, that does not necessarily mean grocery stores are reaping all the benefits. It could be that grocery stores are only able to pass along a fraction of their cost increases to customers, and the place investors should be looking is in a different part of the supply chain.

Some ETFs and mutual funds holding the stocks of companies with a focus on energy, agriculture, and health care are the Van Eck Global Market Vectors Agribusiness ETF, ticker symbol MOO; the State Street Global Advisors Health Care Select Sector SPDR Fund, ticker symbol XLV; the State Street Global Advisors Energy Select Sector SPDR Fund, ticker symbol XLE; the Vanguard Energy Fund Investor Shares, ticker symbol VGENX; and the Fidelity Select Natural Resources Portfolio, ticker symbol FNARX.

Owning the stocks of foreign companies declaring their dividend payments in foreign currencies is a way to consider hedging against inflationary pressures resulting from a falling domestic currency. What I mean by this is finding a foreign company trading on your country's exchanges declaring its dividend first in its domestic currency before converting it to your domestic currency. In fact, you can even combine the strategy of investing in companies that operate in industries from which inflation might emerge with investing in foreign companies declaring dividends in their respective currencies.

With China receiving plenty of attention from investors who believe it is the key to the future of worldwide economic growth, let me provide an example using the Chinese energy giant PetroChina. On U.S. exchanges, investors can gain equity exposure to PetroChina via the company's American Depositary Receipts (ADRs). An ADR is a security that trades on a U.S. exchange, is issued by a bank, and represents a specific number of shares of a foreign stock. PetroChina's board of directors declares the company's dividend in renminbi, currently the official Chinese currency. The declared dividend is then paid out in Hong Kong dollars to holders of PetroChina's H shares. The payment is then converted to U.S. dollars by the bank holding H shares and acting as custodian of PetroChina's ADRs. Then, the dividend is paid in U.S. dollars to ADR shareholders. The shareholders of PetroChina's ADRs will have exposure to the energy industry and the Chinese renminbi.

If you are an investor looking to hedge against inflation resulting from a falling currency, you might consider this type of investment because it provides exposure to foreign currencies without your having to trade foreign currencies. What is particularly interesting about this type of inflation/currency hedging is that when the currency in which the dividend is declared rises against your domestic currency, you do not even need an increase in the stated dividend to get an increase in your yield on cost. Let me provide an example using the French energy giant Total.

Total is a company that declares its dividends in euros. Beginning with the December 2012 quarterly dividend payment, Total's annualized dividend is €2.36 per share. At the moment, €1 is converted to dollars at $1.30. In other words, it costs you $1.30 to obtain €1. If you believe the dollar will fall over time versus the euro, then Total would not even have to increase its dividend for you to realize a rising yield on cost. At a €2.36 dividend per share and a $1.30 exchange rate, the ADR would pay $3.068 per share before taxes. If the euro rises to $1.35, suddenly the ADR would pay $3.186 before taxes without Total's declared dividend ever rising. If the euro rises to $1.45, the dividend would jump to $3.422 before taxes without a rise in Total's declared dividend. As you would expect, if the euro declines versus the dollar, the dollar value of the dividend payout would decline as well.

You may have noticed that in the prior paragraph, I kept stating the ADR's dividend "before taxes." The taxes I was referring to were not the taxes you will pay in your home country, but rather the taxes France will withhold from the dividend. Foreign dividend withholding tax is something investors in the stocks of foreign companies should not forget about. While some countries do not withhold anything from a dividend being paid to foreign investors, others may withhold hefty amounts. It varies across the board, and it can change over time. You should consult each company's website for more information on dividend-withholding rates. Another resource worth consulting is the IRS's "United States Income Tax Treaties – A to Z."

Also, depending on the ADR you own, the agent bank (custodian of the ADRs) may charge an ADR fee, which your broker will deduct from your account. It is typically no more than a few cents per share, per quarter, and is sometimes less than that.

Last, it has become quite popular in recent years to invest in multinational companies deriving revenues from various parts of the globe. The idea behind this is: If the fastest earnings growth will come from non-domestic growth, and you are looking to outpace inflation from a capital appreciation standpoint, you will need exposure to that foreign growth. The technology sector is just one example of a place investors like to park money when trying to capture global growth.

In addition to purchasing the individual stocks or ADRs of companies with a global presence, there are also plenty of funds worth exploring if you are looking to gain overseas exposure. Three such ETFs are the iShares MSCI BRIC Index Fund, ticker symbol BKF; the iShares MSCI Emerging Markets Index Fund, ticker symbol EEM; and the Vanguard MSCI Emerging Markets ETF, ticker symbol VWO. There are scores of other funds worth considering as well, including mutual funds.

Variable/Floating-Rate Bonds; Foreign Currency Denominated Bonds

Besides high-yield bonds, discussed earlier in this chapter, other types of bonds can act as inflation hedges as well. For instance, bonds with variable/floating rates and bonds denominated in a foreign currency can both provide an element of protection against inflation.

Variable/floating-rate bonds include securities such as the new floating-rate Treasuries, first announced in the summer of 2012 (not yet operational at the time this book was published), and step-up bonds. A step-up bond is a bond that pays an increasing coupon over time. Prior to purchasing a variable/floating-rate bond, make sure you clearly understand under what circumstances the yield will adjust. Also, when investing in a variable/floating-rate bond, it is important you are comfortable with the index on which the adjusted rate will be based.

After all, while a variable/floating-rate bond can be great in theory, if the adjustment does not correspond with your inflation experiences, then it will not be an effective hedge for you.

Some investors might consider Treasury Inflation-Protected Securities (TIPS), discussed in Chapter 4, a type of variable/floating-rate security despite the fact that TIPS have fixed interest rates. This is because the principal adjusts according to changes in the Consumer Price Index, thereby creating a variable yield.

Bonds denominated in foreign currencies can also act as an inflation hedge for investors who believe their domestic currency will weaken over time. These types of bonds include those issued by countries and those issued by corporations. If your broker does not provide access to foreign currency bonds, or if you are uncomfortable purchasing individual foreign currency bonds, you can still find exposure to them via exchange-traded products. The table that follows includes several exchange-trade products you might be interested in researching further. Underlying each exchange-traded product, at least a portion of the holdings are non-U.S. dollar based. This includes the Australian dollar, the Canadian dollar, the euro, and more. For a specific breakdown of each product's currency exposure, please visit the website of the sponsor. Also, please remember that the exposure of each fund can change. Just because a fund has exposure to a currency at one time does not mean it will hold that same exposure at a different time.

Table 5.8

Name	Ticker Symbol
PIMCO Australia Bond Index Fund	AUD
PIMCO Canada Bond Index Fund	CAD
State Street Global Advisors SPDR Barclays Capital Emerging Markets Local Bond ETF	EBND
iShares Emerging Markets Local Currency Bond Fund	LEMB
Invesco PowerShares International Corporate Bond Portfolio	PICB
iShares Global ex USD High Yield Corporate Bond Fund	HYXU
Van Eck Global Market Vectors International High Yield Bond ETF	IHY

As with any investment, understanding the risks involved is essential. Two risks to foreign currency denominated bonds are currency risk and no legal recourse. If you own a bond denominated in a foreign currency, it is entirely possible that unfavorable currency market fluctuations could offset all your interest payments and perhaps even more. For example, if you buy a foreign currency denominated bond yielding 5%, and the currency in which that bond is denominated declines by 6%, the drop will have offset an entire year's worth of interest, plus an extra 1%. Also, if you purchase a foreign bond, and the issuer defaults on the debt, it is entirely possible that you will have far less legal recourse, if any, than you would have if a domestic issuer were to default on a bond you held in your account.

Remember that with an inflation hedge, the degree of inflation matters. While some investments may act as solid inflation hedges during times of low-to-moderate inflation, those investments might not work during times of high or out-of-control inflation. While it may seem counterintuitive to purchase a bond as an inflation hedge, depending on the degree of inflation and the yields you can secure, it could be a good decision.

Out-of-the-Money Call Options

It would not surprise me if many investors think that using out-of-the-money call options as an inflation hedge is not worth the time or the money. I would still like to present it because in the event of hyperinflation, out-of-the-money call options can serve a very specific and useful purpose.

The owner of a call option has the right, but not the obligation, to purchase the underlying security at a strike price of his or her choosing. Strike price refers to the price at which the option *owner* has the *right* to buy or sell a security. This is also the price at which the option *seller*, under certain conditions, has the *obligation* to buy or sell a security. An out-of-the-money call option is an option with a strike price far above the current value of the underlying security. For every call option you purchase, you have the right to purchase 100 shares of the underlying security. For example, if you purchase a call option with a strike price of $50 on XYZ stock, you have bought yourself the right to purchase 100 shares of XYZ at $50 per share.

The strategy I will describe involves buying way out-of-the-money call options expiring as far into the future as possible. The purpose of the strategy is to leverage up your portfolio in a cheap way just in case hyperinflation suddenly takes hold. If the strategy works as designed, the increasing value of the call options during hyperinflation will buy you sufficient time to sell other securities in your portfolio and convert them into stores of value.

From a historical basis, it is not unusual for hyperinflation to happen suddenly. Over a period of two to three years, a fiat currency can easily be destroyed. A perhaps less well-known side effect of hyperinflation is that it is not unheard of for stock markets with securities denominated in the currencies being destroyed to soar to unbelievable heights. Germany's and Zimbabwe's hyperinflationary episodes provide two examples of this.

For information on the meteoric climb in Germany's stock market during the hyperinflation of the early 1920s, let's examine Table XII of the "Appendix of Tables" in Costantino Bresciani-Turroni's *The Economics of Inflation*. An index representing the German stock market went from a level of 731 in December 1921 to 8,981 just one year later. It then climbed from 8,981 in December 1922 to 26,890,000,000,000 by December 1923. Of course, the cost of living soared to unbelievable heights as well. But at least Germans investing in the stock market had a fighting chance while the currency lasted.

From December 1921 to October 1922, stock prices in Germany adjusted according to an index of wholesale prices, dropped from 20.97 to 3.64. In other words, the stock market, despite rising 182%, from 731 in December 1921 to 2,062 in October 1922, did not come close to keeping up with inflation during that time. By November 1923, however, stock prices, adjusted according to the same index of wholesale prices, had risen to 32.63. This means that during the worst of the German hyperinflation, equity returns were outpacing wholesale prices in a major way.

Regarding Zimbabwe, Steve H. Hanke and Nicholas Krus' August 15, 2012 Cato Working Paper, "World Hyperinflations," lists Zimbabwe's hyperinflation as reaching a peak in November 2008 at a *daily* inflation rate of 98.0%. In other words, at that time, prices were doubling every 24.7 hours. How does this compare to Weimar Germany's experience? Germany's hyperinflation peaked in October 1923 at a *daily* inflation rate of 20.9%. At that rate, prices were doubling every 3.7 days.

In terms of Zimbabwe's stock market, it is hard to find a lot of details regarding share price performance during the hyperinflation of 2007 and 2008. The various sources available, however, do agree on one thing: The share price performance was spectacular. A January 2, 2008 online article by The China Post mentions the 2007 performance on the Zimbabwe Stock Exchange as being 322,111%. I have also read about returns on the Zimbabwe Stock Exchange topping 200% per day on multiple occasions in October 2008. This was, of course, a time when other stock markets around the world were crashing.

Certainly, there is no guarantee that stock markets would soar in the way Germany's and Zimbabwe's did if hyperinflation were to take hold. Every situation will turn out a bit differently. But there is a case to be made that under hyperinflation, stocks can act as an inflation hedge until the currency completely goes away. It is for this reason that the following strategy can be used as a method to buy you time in the event of hyperinflation. Ideally, it would buy you sufficient time to pull the rest of your assets out of the financial markets and convert them into stores of value.

If you fear the possibility of hyperinflation, consider purchasing far out-of-the-money calls on an equity index such as the S&P 500. The State Street Global Advisors SPDR S&P 500 ETF, ticker symbol SPY, is a popular ETF that seeks to track the performance of the S&P 500. At this time, an investor is able to purchase SPY call options expiring in December 2014, slightly more than two years from now. The $260 December 20, 2014 expiring call option is currently asking 9 cents per contract. There are 125 contracts available at that price. If you purchase all 125 contracts, you will purchase the right to buy 12,500 shares of SPY at $260 each. A price of $260 on SPY equates to roughly 2,600 on the S&P 500. By owning these 125 contracts, you will have acquired exposure to $3,250,000 worth of the SPY (12,500 shares multiplied by $260 per share). This will cost you a total of $1,125, plus a brokerage commission. For $1,125 plus a commission, you have purchased insurance against a hyperinflationary scenario occurring before the end of 2014. Think about how much you will spend in car insurance, homeowners insurance, or health insurance during that time. Is it worth adding another insurance policy to the mix at a cost of a little more than $500 per year?

The $3.25 million of exposure to SPY that you acquired by purchasing the $260 December 20, 2014 calls for 9 cents per contract gives you long exposure to the S&P 500 around a level of 2,600. Today, the index is trading much lower than that. For investors currently long the S&P 500, what would your portfolio be worth if the S&P 500 were to reach 2,600 tomorrow? Would it be worth less than $3.25 million? My guess is that for most investors, it would. Therefore, by purchasing the call options, you would have leveraged up your portfolio, thereby giving yourself a fighting chance to survive hyperinflation should it arise.

The reason to leverage up your portfolio is in case the stock market does not keep up with inflation under a hyperinflationary scenario. By owning exposure to the S&P 500 far in excess of what the remainder of your portfolio would be worth, you have allowed for the possibility that stocks do not keep up with inflation. Hyperinflation could eat away at the $3.25 million of exposure, but as long as that $3.25 million was far in excess of what your portfolio was worth pre-hyperinflation, you have bought yourself time. You thereby also allowed yourself the opportunity to sell the remainder of your investments for whatever they are worth in order to purchase stores of value. Also, there is no need to ever exercise the calls in order to close the option position. That would be a challenge for many investors, as doing so would require a significant amount of money. Instead, you can simply sell the call options in the options market (in whole or in part).

This is not a strategy meant for everyone. This is meant for those individuals who fear hyperinflation and can afford to risk losing the entire premium paid on the call options.

Foreign Currencies

If investing in foreign currencies as an inflation hedge is something that interests you, you can get yourself exposure to a foreign currency in a few different ways. One, you can go to a bank and exchange your currency for a different currency. If you do go to a bank, make sure you find out the fees or markups associated with converting your currency. Many small banks will simply act as a middleman between you and a larger bank, and they will often charge you quite a markup for their service. Wells Fargo is one example of a bank that offers foreign exchange services at competitive prices via the internet, over the phone, or in person. A second way to obtain foreign currency exposure is by trading futures. A third way is to buy an exchange-traded product.

The CurrencyShares ETFs, sponsored by Guggenheim Specialized Products LLC, is a popular exchange-traded method of gaining exposure to foreign currencies. At this time, the following currencies (with ticker symbols) are available for trading through CurrencyShares ETFs: Australian dollar (FXA), British pound sterling (FXB), Canadian dollar (FXC), Chinese renminbi (FXCH), euro (FXE), Japanese yen (FXY), Swedish krona (FXS), and Swiss franc (FXF).

As you decide whether to use currencies as an inflation hedge, think about your ultimate reason for doing so. If the reason is to protect yourself from a currency collapse, ask yourself why you should choose another fiat currency over a store of value such as gold. Perhaps your reason is that you fear confiscation of gold, but you do not fear confiscation of another fiat currency. If you do choose to hedge your domestic fiat currency by purchasing another fiat currency rather than a historical store of value, you should at least be able to come up a solid reason for doing so. On the other hand, if you are purchasing a foreign fiat currency simply to hedge a slow, methodical decline in your domestic currency over a multi-year period, ask yourself why owning the foreign fiat currency is better than owning some of the other investments outlined in this chapter, such as foreign dividend paying equities or foreign currency denominated bonds.

Real Estate

The idea of real estate being an inflation hedge is certainly not unheard of. A real estate purchase is almost certain to be the largest purchase most people will make in their lifetimes. It will also likely end up being the largest single asset most people will own in their lifetimes. First and foremost, I think an ownership stake in a primary residence should be viewed by the occupant(s) as a place to live, a home. Notice I said "ownership stake." The truth is, if you have a mortgage on your home, and the mortgagee (the lender) has the right to kick you out of the home should you fail to pay them a certain sum of money by a certain date, then you do not really own the home. You are really just renting it and continually building a bigger equity stake in it until the day you pay off the loan in its entirety. Even then, after you pay off the mortgage, you will still owe property taxes every year to your municipality. If you do not pay your property taxes, eventually the municipality will foreclose on your home. So again, are you really ever the owner of a property if you have to continually make payments related to the property in order to remain in it?

While we can debate whether homeowners are actually "owners" of a property, the occupant of a home who is current on the mortgage and property taxes definitely is someone with an equity stake in the home. You may have negative equity, or you may have positive equity, but you do have an equity stake in the home. With that equity stake, you can benefit if the property appreciates in value. Therefore, your residence (whether a primary residence or an investment property) does have the capacity to act as an inflation hedge. But just because it has the capacity to act as one does not mean it will.

Have you heard the saying "All real estate is local"? Real estate can easily work as an inflation hedge in some localities and not in others. It truly depends on where you are. You, the occupant with an equity stake, must do your homework on your locality to decide whether it makes sense to work your real estate into your retirement portfolio as an inflation hedge.

In terms of being a store of value, real estate is also often thought of as just that. If you agree with the idea of real estate being a store of value, keep in mind that during times of massive inflation, the property taxes could go up significantly on the real estate in which you have an equity stake. If you cannot afford to pay off those taxes, you will eventually lose the property and your store of value. You will lose the property either by selling it to pay off the taxes or through a foreclosure.

Also, for some people, real estate can act as a source of income and an inflation hedge. The income from renting out real estate in which you have an ownership stake is quite a steady and dependable source of income when tenants are easy to find. Also, the ability to raise those rents can act to protect the purchasing power of that income stream. This is true if you have the pricing power to raise rents by enough to offset the rising costs of maintaining the property and to offset the rising costs of the things on which you spend that income stream.

I must admit that art is not my forte. But I want to include it on this list because I know there are many people who consider it an inflation hedge. While I may not be able to add significant value for art experts with respect to a discussion of art as an inflation hedge, I hope that by sharing the following, my fellow art dilettantes will have something to ponder about art as a viable inflation hedge or store of value.

1. Art is tangible

2. It can be traded in any currency

3. For several centuries, art has been considered a store of value

4. Art is considered an illiquid investment

5. It may be difficult to value certain pieces due to their one-of-a-kind nature

6. Change in tastes could dramatically change valuations

7. Unless you are very wealthy, it can be quite difficult to build a diversified collection of art with a reasonable chance of price appreciation

8. Beware of "chandelier bidding" and dummy bids designed to drive up prices at auctions. A chandelier bid refers to a bid announced by the bid caller when there was no new bid made. It is a tactic used by bid callers in order to keep the bidding alive and the price moving higher. A dummy bidder makes a bid in collusion with the vendor in order to keep the price of the auctioned item moving higher.

* * * * *

Throughout this chapter, I listed a variety of potential inflation hedges and stores of value for a retirement portfolio. Some of the investments described were of the types that distribute no income. It may seem a bit odd to include an asset that distributes no income in a retirement portfolio with an income focus. For some people, it will not make sense to do so. But in other people's portfolios, it will make perfect sense. It all depends on your situation. Your age, asset level, retirement goals, risk tolerance, expenses, and income will all help to shape your portfolio.

I recognize that not all these methods will appeal to everyone. You might find some methods favorable, and you might find others quite unfavorable. Since nobody can predict with certainty the future with respect to inflation, especially 10, 20, or 30 years down the road, a lot of inflation planning involves doing what reasonable expectations would dictate will put the odds in your favor.

Chapter 6

Deflation Protection

Let me start with two questions: First, in any given year, would you rather make 1% or lose 1% on your portfolio? Second, in any given year, would you rather receive a 1% raise or a 1% drop in your income? I am confident most people's answers would be "make 1%" and "a 1% raise." This is because people tend to believe that their financial situations can only improve if the total nominal value of their income and the total value of their assets are rising. But that is simply not true.

What if I told you the 1% loss on the portfolio and the 1% decline in your income came during a year in which the economy experienced deflation of 3%? Furthermore, what if I told you that during the year your portfolio grew by 1% and your income rose by 1%, the economy experienced inflation of 3%? Under those scenarios, on a "real" basis, your purchasing power expanded during the year in which you "lost" money and your purchasing power declined during the year in which you "made" money. By "real," I mean the value of your income or portfolio after adjusting for inflation or deflation.

If your income declines from $50,000 to $49,500 (a 1% decline), but your cost of living drops from $50,000 to $48,500 (a 3% decline), then the real value of your income has increased, despite the nominal value of your income declining. Under that scenario, you went from spending every penny you earned one year to saving $1,000 the next, despite a drop in your income.

Since the Great Depression, as prices have steadily marched ever higher, society as a whole (referring to the United States) has become accustomed to expecting income and investment portfolios to experience ever-rising nominal values. Also, since the Great Depression, the Federal Reserve has actively worked to prevent a repeat of that deflationary period. In recent years, it seems like there is no limit to the amount of unconventional monetary policy (some call it "money printing") the Federal Reserve will employ in an attempt to prevent deflation of asset and consumer prices.

If you believe inflation is the only possible future with respect to price levels, this chapter is likely to be of little interest to you. But if you believe deflationary forces could one day gain a foothold in the economy, or if you feel like the risk of deflation is too great to ignore, then the following list of investment ideas may be of interest:

1. Cash

2. Treasury Bills, Notes, and Bonds

3. High-Quality Investment Grade Corporate Bonds

4. Zero-Coupon Bonds

5. Convertible Bonds

6. Stocks with Yield Support; Consumer Staples, Utilities, Telecom, and Major Drug Manufacturers; Low Beta Stocks

7. Buying and Selling Put Options

8. Stores of Value

Just like we did in Chapter 5, let's tackle this list one at a time.

Cash

There is not a whole lot to say about keeping a portion of your assets in cash if you fear deflation. During deflation, cash, even if it returns 0% on a nominal basis, will have a positive real return. In other words, if you maintain the nominal value of your cash, but your cost of living declines, the real value of your cash will increase.

What exactly am I referring to by "cash"? Do I mean "cold, hard cash" in the traditional sense? When using the word cash, I am referring to money you can hold in your hand as well as deposits at banks. Under a strict definition of the word, cash is actually paper currency and coins. It is also widely accepted, however, that customer deposits held by banks are referred to as cash. This is true despite the fact that banks would be unable to satisfy withdrawal requests if everyone were to pull their money out at once. I also include certificates of deposit (CDs) under the definition of cash because they are technically deposits. But the ability to liquidate your bank CDs and access the deposits will not be as swift as with non-CD bank deposits.

If I were to rank the different levels of cash, I would put "cold, hard cash" at the top, followed by FDIC insured bank deposits, FDIC insured CDs, non-FDIC insured bank deposits, and non-FDIC insured CDs.

Perhaps you are wondering about money market mutual funds. An investment in a money market mutual fund is not a bank deposit and can fluctuate in value. I do not consider money market mutual funds to be cash despite their history of being liquid, safe investments (the year 2008 notwithstanding). Also, do not confuse a money market mutual fund with a money market deposit account. A money market deposit account is considered a bank deposit and generally qualifies for FDIC insurance.

Treasury Bills, Notes, and Bonds

Treasury securities, described in Chapter 4, are an investment to consider when searching for deflation protection. Although Treasuries do not fit strictly within the definition of cash, Treasury bills are considered cash equivalents in today's financial world (as are money market mutual funds). Furthermore, given (1) the role Treasuries play as collateral in the financial markets, (2) the deep, liquid nature of the Treasury market, and (3) a Federal Reserve seemingly ready to crush any Treasury short-sellers in sight, Treasuries have been a go-to asset when investors fear deflation.

In addition, there is generally perceived to be a lack of sufficient non-U.S. government debt considered strong collateral in today's financial system. This means there are very few other places to turn besides U.S. Treasuries when you need to post collateral in a financial transaction. If you are concerned about the possibility of U.S. debt downgrades causing a spike in interest rates, keep this in mind: Should downgrades of U.S. debt occur, it could cause collateral haircuts on Treasury securities, which are used as a major form of collateral in the world's financial system. The great irony of any collateral haircuts on Treasuries is that should investors have no other place to turn for finding collateral to post, the downgrades of U.S. debt could be positive for Treasury prices (higher bond prices means lower bond yields). The reason is that haircuts on Treasuries posted as collateral will only induce more buying of Treasury securities, as investors will need to purchase even more Treasuries just to conduct the same business they did before the haircuts.

A "haircut" refers to the amount that is subtracted from the market value of the security being posted as collateral. If Treasury bills had a haircut of 0.50%, then T-bills with a $1,000,000 market value would be worth $995,000 when posted as collateral for a loan. If collateral haircuts were raised to 1%, it would knock the collateral value of Treasury bills to $990,000. If a bank using Treasuries as a form of collateral had no other options for posting collateral besides Treasuries, the bank would then need to purchase more Treasuries just to conduct the same business it could before, when the haircut was 0.50%. That is one way a downgrade of U.S. debt could actually benefit the Treasury market.

Also, in recent years, Treasury securities, especially intermediate-to long-term Treasuries, have shown a propensity toward a negative correlation with so-called "risk assets." This means that when assets such as stocks and commodities have declined in value, intermediate-to longer-term Treasuries have tended to rally in price (decline in yields).

If you believe risk-asset-price deflation is something worth hedging, Treasury securities have been the go-to asset in recent years. It does not mean they always will be, but for now, "the trend is your friend." Besides buying individual Treasury securities, you also have the option of purchasing funds that track a basket of Treasury securities. A few examples include the iShares Barclays 20+ Year Treasury Bond Fund, ticker symbol TLT; the iShares Barclays 7-10 Year Treasury Bond Fund, ticker symbol IEF; and the Vanguard

Intermediate-Term Treasury Fund Investor Shares, ticker symbol VFITX.

High-Quality Investment Grade Corporate Bonds

Investment grade corporate bonds of the highest quality typically follow the price movements of Treasuries. Under extreme stresses in the economy, there may be a considerable widening of the spreads between the highest quality corporate bonds and Treasuries (like in 2008 and 2009). But in general, these bonds can be expected to track the Treasury securities to which they are benchmarked with only infrequent noteworthy exceptions. Perhaps more importantly, the highest quality corporate bonds are expected to be "money good." In other words, they are expected to fulfill the terms of their debt obligations.

What do I mean by high-quality? First, I am referring to corporate bonds with the highest ratings. This would be those in the triple-A and double-A ratings spectrum. But hopefully the financial crisis of 2008 and 2009 taught fixed income investors that relying on ratings alone is not a prudent way of conducting due diligence on a security. Therefore, beyond credit ratings, I am also referring to businesses that, after performing your assessment of their financial strength, have, in your opinion, virtually no chance of defaulting on their debt. This must be true even in the most difficult times. This would make these types of bonds ideal from an asset protection standpoint in the event of deflation. From a liquidity standpoint, things could be a bit different, especially if deflation is severe. But if you are purchasing individual bonds as a deflation hedge and plan to hold the bonds to maturity, liquidity should be of less concern.

When deciding whether individual bonds or exchange-trade products are the way to go for this deflation hedge, remember that corporate bonds do trade at a spread to Treasuries, and spreads are known to widen during times of asset-price deflation across "risk assets." I included high-quality corporate bonds as a deflation hedge under the assumption that they are money good, not because they are necessarily negatively correlated to things such as high-yield bonds, stocks, or commodities. They might not lose as much money on a mark-to-market basis (relative protection is better than no protection), but if you want to avoid even unrealized losses during deflationary periods, then cash and Treasuries are likely to be more reliable investments.

As a result of the potential for unrealized losses and the lack of a guarantee that the losses will ever be recouped if invested in a fund (perhaps you bought at ultra-low spreads that will never be revisited), I am less inclined to list any available exchange-traded products for this deflation hedge. Individual bonds will eventually mature at par, but bond funds are not guaranteed to return your principal. In a world of deflation, when a return *of* your capital is more important than a return *on* your capital, I would favor individual bonds.

With that said, I understand if some investors are not comfortable building a portfolio of individual bonds. Therefore, I will provide two fixed income exchange-traded products as possibilities to explore. I was not able to find an exchange-traded product that exactly matched the high-quality investment grade corporate bonds I had in mind when writing about this asset as a deflation hedge. I did, however, find two exchange-traded funds that come close.

The iShares Aaa – A Rated Corporate Bond Fund, ticker symbol QLTA, is an ETF that focuses on corporate bonds with ratings above Baa1. The bulk of the fund's bonds are rated below double-A, and it even includes some bonds with ratings below single A. This is a bit lower than I was envisioning for a deflation hedge. But of all the exchange-traded products I looked at, this is the one with the highest ratings profile for corporate bonds. Therefore, I am including it as an idea for further research.

The Guggenheim BulletShares 2020 Corporate Bond ETF, ticker symbol BSCK, is a fixed income ETF that has more concentration in the single-A and triple-B ratings universe than QLTA. The defining feature for this fund is that it is a defined maturity ETF. This means it is designed to track the performance of a held-to-maturity portfolio of investment grade corporate bonds, adding an element of "return *of* capital" that other investment grade corporate bond products lack. That is why I am including it as an idea for further research.

On a final note, you may have noticed I did not mention the popular iShares iBoxx $ Investment Grade Corporate Bond Fund, ticker symbol LQD. I favored iShares' QLTA over LQD because

QLTA came closer to meeting the credit rating requirements I envision for this deflation hedge. Concerning Guggenheim's BSCK, although LQD and BSCK had more similar credit rating profiles, I favored Guggenheim's fund due to its defined maturity.

Please remember that I conducted only a cursory overview of various funds in order to find a few products that met some of the basic criteria I was envisioning for this deflation hedge. Upon performing a more thorough review of these ETFs, you might discover that none of them is to your liking. They are merely a starting point for your further due diligence.

Zero-Coupon Bonds

Zero-coupon bonds are bonds that do not have coupons and therefore do not make interest payments. Instead, they are issued at a discount to their face value and pay out the face value as one lump sum payment at maturity. Zero-coupon bonds are a useful tool for planning for future expenses because they allow you to know exactly how much money an investment will provide on a specific date, assuming the issuer does not default on the bond. Since the imputed interest is compounded over the life of the zero-coupon bond, it allows you to definitively know at what rate your "interest" is to be reinvested. Imputed interest refers to interest you are considered to have received, even though no interest was actually received. This contrasts with a traditional bond paying simple interest. In that case, the investor does receive interest payments and would need to reinvest those payments.

Why did I include zero-coupon bonds on the list of potential deflation hedges? The compounding effect of zero-coupon bonds allows you to "reinvest" the imputed interest at a set yield. Therefore, if you believe interest rates for the issuer of the bond in which you are investing will decline during times of deflation, the zero-coupon bond gives you the opportunity to essentially lock in a higher rate for the reinvestment of the imputed interest. This means the reinvestment risk of the non-principal portion of a zero-coupon bond is taken out of the equation. That is a good thing in a falling-rate environment. Reinvestment risk refers to the risk of interest rates being lower than they were when you made the original investment when the time comes to reinvest interest payments or principal. In that case, you would have to decide whether to reinvest at the lower rate or not reinvest at all.

One difficulty of investing in zero-coupon bonds is that you are required to pay income taxes on imputed interest each year, despite not having received any interest payments from the bond. For tax purposes, this type of "interest" is known as original issue discount (OID). On a zero-coupon bond, OID is the excess of the bond's stated redemption price over the issue price. In the case of a stripped bond or stripped coupon, the OID is the excess of the bond's stated redemption price over the price at which you acquired it. There are other things to consider when calculating taxes for OID purposes. IRS Publication 1212, "Guide to Original Issue Discount (OID) Instruments," and IRS Publication 550, "Investment Income and Expenses," are two resources worth consulting for more details on original issue discount taxation.

If you find zero-coupon bonds of interest but are nervous about having to pay taxes on "phantom income," you might be happy to hear the following three ways of reducing the tax hit on imputed interest:

1. Hold the zero-coupon bond in a tax-deferred or tax-free account, such as a Traditional IRA or Roth IRA. You might even consider doing this with zero-coupon bonds that have tax exemptions. It is true that conventional wisdom says you do not want to hold bonds with tax exemptions in IRAs. But here is one exception to that rule: If you believe a bond with a tax exemption, such as a municipal bond, will outperform taxable investments you would otherwise make in your IRA, then holding the tax-exempt bond in an IRA is acceptable. After all, why would you give up purchasing an asset with returns superior to another's just because conventional wisdom says you should not hold that asset in an IRA? In recent years, it has not been uncommon to see federally tax-exempt municipal bonds yielding more than federally taxable Treasuries. In some cases, investors could have even found municipal bonds with acceptable credit risk profiles yielding more than federally taxable high-quality corporate bonds. This is just one example illustrating why it is often a good idea to spend some

time questioning whether conventional wisdom is correct as it pertains to investing.

2. Zero-coupon municipal bonds are a way to reduce the tax liability on imputed interest since municipal bonds are exempt from federal taxation. Furthermore, if you purchase a zero-coupon muni from the state in which you reside, there is a good chance the bond will be exempt from all taxation. This is because munis from the state in which you live are not only exempt from federal income taxes but are often exempt from state and local income taxes as well. One note of caution: There has been plenty of noise out of Washington, D.C. with respect to reducing or eliminating the federal tax exemption that municipal bonds currently enjoy. Investors should follow this issue closely.

3. Zero-coupon Treasury securities are the third way to reduce the tax hit on "phantom income." It is often overlooked that interest earned on Treasury securities enjoys a state and local income tax exemption. Therefore, if you purchase a U.S. Treasury zero-coupon bond, you will not have to pay state or local income taxes on "phantom income."

Convertible Bonds

Convertible bonds are securities with both stock-like and bond-like features. In essence, they are bonds that can be converted into shares of a company's stock at the discretion of the bondholder. But that discretion does come with an exception. Companies can attempt to force a conversion to stock by calling the convertible bond. But bondholders have the right to redeem their bonds at the call price rather than converting the bonds to stock.

What follows are three examples of circumstances that may cause a convertible bond to be called: when interest rates have declined significantly, if a company wants to retire debt, and if the price of the stock is above the conversion price. The number of shares into which the bond can be converted is predetermined. The price at which the bond can be converted is also predetermined and typically expressed either as an explicitly stated price or as a premium to the price of the stock at the time the bond was issued.

In general, convertible bonds are known for having lower interest rates than other bonds from the same company. This is because the convertible bondholder has upside exposure to the equity. If the stock goes higher, that is a good thing for the convertible bondholder. Owners of convertible bonds who are worried about possible deflation in asset prices might prefer to look at the bond as a type of stock with a put option attached to it. The owner of a put option has the right, but not the obligation, to sell the underlying security at a certain price. In a deflationary situation, a put option can be a very valuable thing to own. In the case of a convertible bond, the "put" is basically the fact that the bond will mature at par or, if called, redeemed at the call price. This protects you from the downside of falling equity prices.

It is important to note that I have been referring to plain vanilla convertibles. There are many different types of convertible bonds, and some might not be appropriate as deflation hedges. You should certainly read the indenture of any convertible bond you are interested in purchasing to learn all the pertinent details.

Pure play convertible bond exchange-traded products are a relatively new phenomenon; the first ETF focused solely on the convertible bond market debuted in April 2009. That first convertible bond ETF, the State Street Global Advisors SPDR Barclays Capital Convertible Securities ETF, ticker symbol CWB, currently attempts to track the performance of the "Barclays Capital U.S. Convertible Bond >$500 MM Index." Prior to CWB's inception, investors wanting convertible bond ETF exposure needed to look at preferred stock ETFs that also held some convertible bonds. Since CWB's debut, another convertible bond ETF began trading: the Invesco PowerShares Convertible Securities Portfolio, ticker symbol CVRT. It currently seeks to replicate the performance of the "BofA Merrill Lynch All U.S. Convertibles Index."

For investors interested in non-ETF, non-individual securities products, there are a number of convertible bond mutual funds available. I would suggest talking to a representative at your mutual fund provider about which convertible funds are available for their clients to purchase. Two examples of such funds from two of the largest mutual fund providers are the Vanguard Convertible Securities

Fund, ticker symbol VCVSX, and the Fidelity Convertible Securities Fund, ticker symbol FCVSX.

I would like to caution investors considering convertible bond investing through funds rather than through individual securities that the deflation protection with respect to convertible bonds comes from the fact that bondholders can hold the bonds to maturity. By having the option to hold a convertible bond to maturity and having the principal returned in full, the convertible bond investor is protected in a way that the convertible bond fund investor is not. Remember that a fund tracks the performance of an index. By attempting to follow the index, a fund might sell securities for a loss that you would have held to maturity. The fund, by attempting to track an index, might never return to the level at which you purchased it. You, however, by holding an individual, non-defaulted bond to maturity, will get back the face value of the bond regardless of how low the security traded at one time or another.

One final note regarding convertible bonds: Some investors argue that due to the upside exposure to a company's stock, convertible bonds are also an inflation hedge. While they would act as an inflation hedge for a portfolio heavily tilted toward bonds, I do not think they would be as strong an inflation hedge for a more diversified portfolio. Therefore, I left convertible bonds off the list of inflation hedges in Chapter 5. With that said, there may be some investors with portfolios heavily tilted toward bonds who may want to consider convertible bonds as inflation hedges.

Stocks with Yield Support; Consumer Staples, Utilities, Telecom, and Major Drug Manufacturers; Low Beta Stocks

Owning stocks during periods of deflation can be brutal for a portfolio. You will need to decide whether the risk of deflation is so great that you need to exit all investments that might flounder during it, or whether the risk is such that your portfolio simply needs to be hedged for it. If the answer is to hedge your portfolio, then one possibility is to consider stocks with yield support. Stocks with yield support refer to those providing dividend yields large enough that investors will be drawn to them during difficult economic times and during times when bond yields are low. This does not mean the stocks will avoid falling in price; the idea is that higher yields will help offset some of the declines.

As the yield on the 10-year Treasury note dropped below that of the S&P 500 in 2011, it was not uncommon to hear investing professionals say the S&P 500 had yield support. I do not buy the argument that just because the S&P 500 yields even as much as 0.75% more than a 10-year Treasury, it gives the broad market index yield support. The S&P 500's dividend yield is still quite low, both in nominal terms and on a historical basis. From my perspective, an S&P 500 dividend yield of below 2.25% does not give it much yield support, even when the 10-year Treasury is yielding less. Instead, when searching for yield support, I like to focus on companies with dividends in the 3% to 7% range.

As an aside, you might be wondering why I put a cap on the range. When I start seeing dividends on individual stocks abnormally higher than the rest of the market, I start to ask myself whether the company can really afford to pay that kind of dividend on a sustained basis. Often times, the answer is no. In the era of ultra-low interest rates (in the U.S.), an ultra-high dividend yield should have potential new investors in that company's stock asking the question why it is that other investors have not jumped on board, bringing the dividend yield back down in line with its peers. Don't get me wrong; there are times when stocks yielding 7% or more are a buy. But caution is warranted when you come across abnormally high dividend yields.

Furthermore, during times of deflation, if you are finding stocks with high single-digit or even double-digit yields, it is likely because the stock price itself has fallen precipitously. In that case, the market would not be sending the best message about that company's future business prospects. The bottom line: Do not get lured by ultra-high dividend yields solely because of the yield.

The following should go without saying, but I will state it anyway. Just because I like to focus on stocks in the 3% to 7% dividend range when looking for stocks with yield support does not mean the dividend yield is the sole determinant of whether the stock will have yield support. A company's overall business strength must be perceived by the market to be able to withstand difficult economic times relatively well in order for investors to be willing to take the risk of buying the stock. Once you find companies that pass that test (the fundamental research), you can start choosing among them the stocks likely to have yield support. When looking for companies whose businesses are often perceived to hold up well during difficult economic times and during asset-price deflation, investors tend to flock to consumer staples. Companies in that sector are thought of as benefitting from people's *needs*, which, in theory, should support revenues during difficult economic times more so than products that satisfy people's *wants*.

When looking at the performance of the consumer staples sector during each of the last two bear markets in stocks, the State Street Global Advisors Consumer Staples Select Sector SPDR Fund, ticker symbol XLP, serves as a good proxy. It declined 38.29% and 36.35% respectively, peak-to-trough, excluding dividends, during the 2000 to 2002 and 2007 to 2009 bear markets. The S&P 500, on the other hand, declined 50.51% and 57.69% during each of the past two bear markets, peak-to-trough, excluding dividends.

Many people like to use the Dow Jones Industrial Average as the gauge for the overall stock market. I prefer to use broader indices rather than an index with just 30 stocks. With that said, the Dow did perform in line with consumer staples during the 2000 to 2002 bear market, falling "just" 38.75% peak-to-trough, excluding dividends. During the 2007 to 2009 bear market, however, the Dow got beat up just like the other broader indices, falling 54.43%.

Other sectors investors like to look to for yield support include utilities and telecommunications. While the yields may be supportive in the sense of offsetting some of the unrealized capital losses, these sectors did not perform nearly as well as consumer staples did during each of the past two bear markets. For example, the State Street Global Advisors Utilities Select Sector SPDR Fund, ticker symbol XLU, dropped 56.87% and 49.66% respectively during the 2000 to 2002 and 2007 to 2009 bear markets. One interesting thing to note about XLU during those bear markets is that it topped out roughly eight months later than the S&P 500 in the year 2000 and two months later in 2007. Using XLU as a proxy for utilities, investors were indeed treating the sector as a safe haven *early on* in those bear markets.

The telecom sector got absolutely destroyed during the 2000 to 2002 and the 2007 to 2009 bear markets, underperforming both the S&P 500 and the Dow Jones Industrial Average. Nevertheless, telecom has thus far been a go-to place in this low-interest-rate environment.

Given today's historically low interest rates and the fact that many investors are desperately searching for yield, it is difficult to know how consumer staples, utilities, and telecom will perform during the next bear market. Any pullbacks in the stocks of companies believed to be able to continue paying healthy dividends may be viewed as buying opportunities. I cannot emphasize enough, however, that owning stocks during a deflationary period in the economy or during a bear market in stocks, regardless of the sector from which the stocks come, is almost always a relative performance game. Practically all stocks end up going down, but investors try to outperform the market on a relative basis by finding places to hide.

Given that I just spent some time discussing sectors selling goods and services characterized by people's needs rather than people's wants (telecom is certainly debatable), you might be wondering why I did not include the health care sector on the list. After all, the health care sector, as measured by the State Street Global Advisors Health Care Select Sector SPDR Fund, ticker symbol XLV, "only" declined 36.24% during the bear market of the early 2000s and 42.91% during the 2007 to 2009 bear market. In both cases, this outperformed the S&P 500.

As is widely known, in the United States, the future liabilities to which the government is subject, due to promises made through health insurance for senior citizens and low income households, is so great that I have no idea what the health care sector will even look like ten or more years down the road. With a future liability for health care as large as that of the U.S. government's, there is no telling what measures the government will resort to in an attempt to solve its problems. But given the unsustainable path of the government's future medical liabilities, action will eventually have to be taken.

How these unpredictable measures will affect the profitability of the health care sector is anyone's guess. Over the coming years, I imagine there could be a good amount of volatility in the businesses of health insurance providers and hospital operators. Therefore, unless you are looking to hold those types of companies' stocks for shorter periods of time, or unless you have a unique insight into how the sector will look many years down the road, it may be better to look elsewhere for deflation hedges.

If you are not concerned about the impact of potential changes to health care laws in the years ahead and are intrigued by the aforementioned health care ETF, ticker symbol XLV, you should be aware of the following information: Despite the fact that XLV had over fifty holdings as of September 27, 2012, just three companies (the major drug manufacturers Johnson & Johnson, Pfizer, and Merck) had a collective weighting of approximately 33% of the fund, and the top 10 holdings had a collective weighting of approximately 60% of the fund. Furthermore, slightly over 50% of the fund's allocation was categorized as "Pharmaceuticals." These are all things to keep in mind when thinking about how diversified you would like your health care exposure to be.

Owning low-beta stocks is another way to potentially outperform on a relative basis during periods of asset-price deflation. Concerning stocks, beta describes the volatility of a stock's price in relation to the volatility of a corresponding index, such as the S&P 500. The index used in comparison has a beta of one. If a stock's beta is higher than one, it tends to move in the same direction as the index to which it is being compared, but it moves in greater amounts. A beta of less than one but greater than zero indicates a stock that tends to move less than the market does on any given day. The closer the beta gets to zero, the less correlated a stock's price is to the overall market. The more a stock's beta moves into negative territory, the more the stock's price tends to be negatively correlated to the index to which it is being compared.

For example, over time, a stock with a beta of two should rise and fall by twice the amount of the index to which it is compared. If the index rises 1%, the stock with a beta of two should rise 2%. Similarly, over time, a stock with a beta of negative two should also be twice as volatile as the index to which it is compared. But rather than move in the same direction as the index, it should move in the opposite direction.

If you are looking to hedge your equity portfolio from asset-price deflation, focusing on stocks (or other assets for that matter) with betas below one can, in theory, help you achieve this. There are plenty of stocks among the utilities, consumer staples, telecoms, and major drug manufacturers that have betas between zero and one.

More aggressive investors might purchase inverse exchange-traded products when trying to capture negative beta over shorter periods of time. Inverse exchange-traded products are securities that are designed to move in the opposite direction of an asset or index. One such example is the ProShares Short S&P 500 ETF, ticker symbol SH. But when trading inverse ETFs, remember that they are securities designed to be used for shorter periods of time. As ProShares notes on its website, "This Short ProShares ETF seeks a return that is -1x the return of an index or other benchmark (target) FOR A SINGLE DAY, as measured from one NAV calculation to the next. Due to the compounding of daily returns, ProShares' returns over periods other than one day will likely differ in amount and possibly direction from the target return for the same period."

If inverse ETFs are not to your liking, you might also consider Treasury securities when searching for negative beta. It is not uncommon for intermediate- to long-term Treasuries to exhibit negative beta relative to broad stock market indices.

Keep in mind that looking at beta is but one element of finding a deflation hedge, and beta does not measure the risk of a company's business performing poorly. There are likely to be some really horrible investments with betas less than one. Using beta as one determinant in finding a deflation hedge for your portfolio does not substitute for fundamental research of the business in which you are considering investing.

Buying and Selling Put Options

As I mentioned in the convertible bonds section, during deflation, put options can be a very valuable thing to own. This is because the owner of a put option has the right, but not the obligation, to sell an asset at a certain price (the strike price). If prices are declining, and you own a put option that allows you to sell an asset at a higher price than that asset is currently trading, that is a good thing. Think of it as a type of insurance against falling prices. Naturally, you will not get a put option for free. There are premiums to be paid when purchasing any type of insurance, and put options are no different. Therefore, buying put options is a strategy best suited for individuals who are confident in their abilities to determine whether the probability of falling asset prices is high enough and whether the potential drop of asset prices is large enough to justify the cost of the insurance (the put option).

When selling a put option, you have the obligation to purchase an asset at a particular price if you are assigned the shares. While selling puts is not a deflation hedge per se, it is an alternative way for a long-only stock investor to invest during periods of falling asset prices.

Rather than owning stocks outright during deflationary periods, a long-only investor could consider selling out-of-the-money puts and attempt to collect option premiums without ever having to own the underlying asset. When using this strategy, however, the put seller does run the risk of being forced to purchase the underlying security. After all, as a put seller, you are obligated to purchase the underlying security if an options assignment takes place. Typically, you are only assigned the shares if the security's price declines below the strike price you chose to sell. As a review, the strike price refers to the price at which an option *owner* has the *right* to buy or sell an asset. This is also the price at which an option *seller*, under certain conditions, has the *obligation* to buy or sell an asset.

Regarding selling puts and possibly being assigned shares of the underlying asset, let's look at an example: If you sell a $10 put option on XYZ stock, and the stock closes at $10.20 on the date the option expires, the chances of you being assigned shares of XYZ are very small. This is because it would not make sense for the owner of the stock to sell it to you for $10 when he or she could sell it in the open market for $10.20. By taking on the risk of having to purchase shares at the strike price of your choosing, you collect a premium from the put buyer. In effect, you are acting as the insurance provider for the person to whom you sold the put option.

During a period of deflation, it might make sense for some investors to consistently sell out-of-the-money put options at prices below current market values in an attempt to continually collect premiums without ever having to own the underlying security. An out-of-the-money put option is an option with a strike price below the current price of the underlying security. As long as you choose a strike price at which you would not mind owning the security, your worst case scenario is that you are forced to buy it at a price lower than its current market value.

Trading options is certainly not for everybody. Before trading options, I would highly suggest visiting one of the many websites on the internet that explains options in great detail. There are also numerous books available for purchase that explain options in great detail.

Stores of Value

At the beginning of this chapter, I never defined deflation. In Chapter 5, however, I did define inflation as "a rise in prices for the things we buy." Therefore, one might intuitively assume that an acceptable definition of deflation is the opposite: a fall in prices for the things we buy. While this does seem to be a suitable definition of deflation in terms of its relevance to people, there is a more esoteric way of looking at deflation. It involves stores of value.

In Chapter 5, I discussed stores of value as a different type of inflation hedge. Stores of value act as a bridge from one currency regime to another. Gold is widely considered the ultimate store of value. Depending on your point of view, various stores of value, but especially gold, can act as deflation hedges as well. This is because at the end of a fiat currency collapse, everything *deflates* in price relative to stores of value.

You might become a billionaire or trillionaire during a fiat currency collapse, and the price of gold, silver, or any other store of value might lag in terms of its nominal value in the failing currency. But once the end of the fiat currency arrives, that currency loses all value and is no longer used for the payment of goods and services. Stores of value, however, live on. They can be converted to whatever new money comes about. Those stores of value might not realize their true value until the currency collapse is complete, but eventually their true worth is recognized. Stores of value allow people to carry over wealth from one system of money to the next. It is hard to put a fiat currency value on that.

If we look at deflation from the more standard point of view of falling prices, stores of value are not immune from falling in terms of their fiat currency prices. Stores of value such as gold might outperform on a relative basis by declining less than other assets, but they certainly can and often will decline in price at times.

So why is it that I include stores of value under both the inflation and deflation chapters of this book? Depending on your point of view, they can be either an inflation hedge or a deflation hedge. Whether you assess the stores of value in a fiat currency being devalued, a soon-to-be new fiat currency, or simply as objects that have value, your perspective will help determine whether you view them as an inflation hedge or a deflation hedge. You might even view them as both. The bottom line is that stores of value are stores of value. They provide a type of protection that transcends any type of protection afforded by investments that pay out in fiat currencies.

* * * * *

As I conclude Part II of this book, I would like to remind investors that hedging is not necessarily about eliminating your risk. It is about helping to *reduce* your risk. Hedging will not always prevent you from suffering losses, but it can help you limit those losses. Hedging will sometimes prevent you from realizing all the upside from an investment, but it will also help you avoid all the downside. One way to think of a portfolio hedge is as an insurance policy. If you are an investor heavily focused on income at the expense of capital appreciation, you may want to search for hedges that should help protect the purchasing power of your portfolio. On the other hand, if you are heavily invested in equities and wish to hedge the risk of deflation crushing the value of your investments, you might consider hedges that will protect your principal. Or you might simply consider certain allocations within equities that have less volatility, pay higher dividends, and are generally favored by investors during difficult economic times.

I have presented a lot of different ideas about hedging a portfolio against inflation, deflation, and currency collapse. The extent of the list was not to imply that you should use all of them or even most of them when constructing your retirement portfolio. I simply hope that when you encounter certain challenges over your investing lifetime, you will now be armed with enough ideas and knowledge to help you feel comfortable either discussing the challenges with your investment advisor or taking them on yourself.

Part III

Investing Considerations Not to Be Overlooked

Conventional wisdom refers to generally-accepted truths that many people adhere to without ever questioning the validity of those "truths." A non-investing-related example is to change your car's oil every 3,000 miles. In the world of investing, conventional wisdom is a dominating force. One example is the widespread belief that "buy-and-hold" is the path to investing success. Another example is the idea that when you are younger, you should have a higher allocation to stocks, and when you are older, the allocation should shift to bonds. A third example is the idea of keeping your emotions out of investing.

This part of the book addresses the final two of the five fundamentals of building a retirement portfolio and also provides perspectives on a variety of topics. At times, these perspectives will challenge conventional wisdom.

Chapter 7

Liquidity

Making sure you are invested in assets with sufficient liquidity to suit your needs is incredibly important when constructing a retirement portfolio. This is especially true given the fact that most investors will not be able to live solely off the income produced by a portfolio but will instead need to draw down the principal at some point.

Liquidity is perhaps best known as the ease with which an asset can quickly be purchased or sold without affecting the price of that asset. Can you sell 50,000 shares of a stock in the blink of an eye at the current bid without causing big moves in a security's price? Or will selling 50,000 shares into the market knock the security's price down 2%? Can you raise cash quickly and at a reasonable price given the assets in your portfolio, or will it take days, weeks, or perhaps even months to move to cash (such as with real estate, for example)? The answers to these types of questions help give an indication of the liquidity of a security or a portfolio.

Hidden Liquidity

Securities with wide bid-ask spreads are often thought of as illiquid. But that is not necessarily the case. There is lots of hidden liquidity in the financial markets, and securities with wide bid-ask spreads may have hidden liquidity between the bid and ask prices. What I mean by hidden liquidity is liquidity that is *hidden from the investing public.* For instance, if you are following a Level II screen, which shows the current bid-ask prices and bid-ask sizes displayed by various market makers, you will not necessarily see all the *best* prices at which market participants are currently willing to trade.

Even stocks trading with one penny spreads between the bid and ask prices will have orders executed within that spread with liquidity that was hidden. On numerous occasions, I have entered orders to purchase stocks and had those orders filled below the supposed best offer price. It has also happened to me in the options market, where spreads can often be quite wide on low-volume strike prices. If you use limit orders and try to get filled between the supposed best bid and best ask, you might be surprised by the outcome. You will not always get an order filled between the bid and ask prices, but it is not unusual for it to happen. If you are interested in trying this out, let me offer this tip: If you want to purchase a security, the closer you are to the advertised asking price, the better chance you will have of finding liquidity. If you want to sell a security, the closer you are to the advertised bid, the better chance you will have of finding liquidity.

For example, if a bid-ask spread on an option is $0.30 by $0.37, and you want to sell that option, consider starting your bid at $0.33 (using a limit order). If you do not get any bites after a couple of minutes, consider moving it to $0.32, and so on. Of course, if you are worried about the market moving quickly, and you just want to get filled, you can always accept the bid and sell the option for $0.30.

Another example is the following: Let's say you want to purchase a stock bidding $10.50 and asking $10.53. Conventional wisdom tells us that you buy at the offer price (the "ask") and sell at the bid. In this case, however, if I were not too anxious to purchase the stock, I would consider entering a buy limit order at $10.52. There have even been times when I have had buy orders filled on the *bid*, and the stock actually went higher immediately thereafter. The conventional rules of the market indicate that should not happen, but it is nice to benefit from it when it does.

As an aside, a limit order is an order that indicates the worst price you are willing to accept. On a buy limit order, you specify the highest price at which you are willing to buy. On a sell limit order, you specify the lowest price at which you are willing to sell. Limit orders offer you some control over the price at which your order will be executed. This contrasts with a market order, which gives control to the market maker. A market order is supposed to be filled at the next best current price. But in the world of lightning-fast computer trading, when using a market order, the best bid or offer in the market at the time you enter your order might be quite different from the price at which you end up getting filled. That is not always the case, but if you are considering using market orders, you need to be aware of the fact that prices can suddenly change *very quickly*.

On a final note, while wide spreads do not necessarily indicate a lack of liquidity in a security, they do represent higher transaction costs for trading a security. This is because investors who do not search for hidden liquidity are often buying and selling at prices higher and lower than those at which they need to.

Essentially, there are no hard-and-fast rules when it comes to finding hidden liquidity. I am simply offering insights from my experiences in the market, which can help you think through how to approach finding hidden liquidity, if that is something that interests you.

Market Depth and Volume

Market depth is also a determinant of liquidity in the minds of many market participants. But in today's day and age with high-frequency trading and dark pools (institutional orders hidden from the public) dominating the markets, what you believe to be market depth might not be. Market depth refers to the balance of available pending shares (or other securities) for purchase and sale. Securities with imbalances between the number of shares available for purchase and the number of shares available for sale are susceptible to being moved in one direction or another. A security with a lack of market depth is often referred as being illiquid. But a security with market depth is not necessarily liquid. This is because the presence of market depth does not tell you whether the depth is what I like to call "real."

When discussing liquidity, it is important not to confuse volume with liquidity. Despite the fact that the words volume and liquidity are often used interchangeably, volume does *not* equal liquidity. The 'Flash Crash' of May 6, 2010 was an extremely high volume day across the financial markets, yet I doubt many investors would characterize that day as one known for liquidity.

The depth of a market is a more realistic gauge of liquidity than volume is, but even market depth as it is traditionally understood is not the best measure of liquidity. In years gone by, volume and market depth might have been more realistic gauges of liquidity. Nowadays, however, markets are dominated by lightning-fast computer programs and dark pools, which make it very difficult to know what the "real" market depth is. I define "real" market depth as the level of liquidity on which you can depend during adverse market conditions. This "real" market depth is a much closer definition of liquidity than the definition you will normally hear.

It is widely assumed that the U.S. financial markets are very liquid. They are certainly much more so than in other parts of the world. This is especially true for the stock market. What this widely held view fails to recognize, however, is that liquidity during stable times does not equal liquidity during unstable times. For example, are the bids that we see during stable times real in that they are part of genuine market making activities? Or are the open buy orders (the bids) there for some other reason, only to be pulled during times of market stress?

If the idiosyncrasies and inner-workings of the stock market interest you, consider researching the following terms, the details of which are beyond the scope of this book: liquidity rebates, high-frequency trading, dark pools, quote stuffing, co-location, and low latency. To summarize, just because an entity is making a market does not mean it will make that market when financial markets are in turmoil. To support this point, let's briefly discuss what happened during the 'Flash Crash' of 2010.

Flash Crash

The financial markets gave us all a glimpse of the true market depth for thousands of securities during the 'Flash Crash' on May 6, 2010. On that day, the Dow Jones Industrial Average declined by 9.19% intraday, and the S&P 500 declined by 8.59% intraday before recovering a good chunk of those losses within minutes. When briefly examining the charts of various stocks, ETFs, and ETNs from that day, investors can see the true extent of the market depth for various securities.

During the 'Flash Crash,' many securities plunged well more than the eight to ten percent declines experienced by the major indices. In fact, some stocks and exchange-traded products plunged by 99% or more, trading for just pennies, before quickly rebounding. And soon thereafter, the exchanges would forever erase some of these "erroneous" trades from the record books, canceling many of the trades that resulted in securities plunging to, in some cases, just one penny.

Investors who were fortunate enough to have buy orders executed during the massive declines on May 6, and then sold later that day for a large profit, would soon become quite unfortunate. As they learned, if your order to buy a security is deemed erroneous, but you sold the security before finding out your buy order was retroactively deemed erroneous, you will suddenly find yourself short that security. Imagine being an everyday investor who thought he or she bought and then sold a stock for a profit, only to find out the next morning that the buy order was cancelled, but the sell order was not. Suddenly, you went from thinking you had a profit on a long position to being short that security.

While the exchanges erased from the record books many of the deepest declines in stocks and exchange-traded products from May 6, 2010, not all the major declines were expunged from history. Procter & Gamble is one example of a popular company whose stock plunged during the 'Flash Crash.' When looking at a candlestick chart of Procter & Gamble's stock from that day, one can clearly see that the stock, which closed at $62.16 on May 5, traded as low as $39.37 on May 6, before closing at $60.75. The long tail on Procter & Gamble's candlestick chart shows the stress the stock was under that day. The greater than 36% drop in the stock on no news worthy of that sort of move was not normal and provides insight into the true depth of the market as it pertains to Procter & Gamble's stock.

An example of an ETF that experienced severe stress on May 6, 2010 is the iShares S&P 500 Growth Index Fund, ticker symbol IVW. On May 5, 2010, this fund closed at $59.52. The following day, during the crash, it plunged to $25 per share, a decline of roughly 58%, before rebounding and closing at $57.67. A candlestick chart of IVW clearly shows this move. Remember, IVW is an exchange-traded fund. It routinely has a few hundred holdings, including the stocks of companies like Apple, Exxon Mobil, International Business Machines, Microsoft, Chevron, and Google. A 58% decline in one day should not happen to that type of fund.

There are plenty of other exchange-traded products that fell into the same boat as IVW that day. There are also plenty of other stocks besides Procter & Gamble that had liquidity issues on May 6, 2010. I chose them randomly to serve as examples and not for any other reasons. On the day of the 'Flash Crash,' the "real" market depth of the U.S. stock market was exposed as some electronic market makers shut down operations during the crash, and liquidity dried up.

I will leave historians to debate what actually caused the crash. I am more interested in the market structure that could ever facilitate such a thing. Advances in technology have changed the structure of the financial markets and changed the way in which investors should think about liquidity. Today's market structure is such that a small number of high-frequency traders control a very large share of the overall daily volume and market depth. Those high-frequency traders also act as market makers and operate on very thin margins. With this in mind, it should not surprise anyone that a liquidity-crushing event could happen.

* * * * *

To conclude the discussion on liquidity, I would like to briefly focus on it in a way that many people might not think to. Liquidity is often viewed from a more micro level in portfolio management. Is this investment or that security liquid? I agree with the importance of examining the liquidity of a portfolio's individual components. But there is another element to the overall liquidity of a portfolio you should also consider, especially when you do not handle the day-to-day responsibilities of managing your money.

If your money is invested with a company that has a set of rules about when, how often, and under what conditions withdrawals can be made, you must take that into consideration when thinking about liquidity. Liquidity is not just important from the perspective of how quickly and at what price you can turn a stock or a bond into cash, but it is also important from the perspective of how quickly can you get access to money in the portfolio if you so choose.

Should a company managing your money only allow withdrawals once per month or once per quarter, your overall liquidity is constrained. If you must provide notice weeks in advance of a withdrawal, not only is your liquidity constrained, but you have also lost the ability to take withdrawals at the optimal time for your portfolio. Instead of being able to take withdrawals at favorable times, you will be forced to guess whether a redemption made weeks from when you put the request in will occur at favorable prices. Finally, consider how you might get by if your hedge fund's prime broker experiences difficulties and freezes withdrawals. If you put in a withdrawal request to your hedge fund, but the hedge fund cannot get the money from the prime broker, you are most likely not getting the money either.

In closing, remember not to focus solely on the individual securities in your portfolio when thinking about the portfolio's liquidity. Take a step back and look at the big picture, i.e., the speed of converting "cash" sitting in the portfolio to cash at your fingertips. Finally, as a market participant, remember to work multiple assumptions about liquidity into your portfolio planning depending on a variety of possible market conditions.

Chapter 8

Principal Preservation

Principal preservation is an important element of any retirement portfolio. The principal of your portfolio refers to the original amount of money invested. In the case of retirement, I am defining principal as the amount of money with which you begin your retirement. My definition of principal does not adjust for inflation or deflation. Maintaining the purchasing power of your portfolio is also important and is addressed when you do your inflation and deflation planning as part of building your retirement portfolio. For the purposes of this chapter, I am addressing principal from a nominal value perspective with a focus on how to allocate the money to protect the original starting value from movements in the financial markets.

Your principal is essentially the source of your investment income and is therefore incredibly important to manage in a way that makes it last for as long as possible. A decision to draw down your principal should not be made lightly. As I mentioned a few times in this book, I understand that most investors will need to draw down their principal in retirement. This needs to be done in a way that ensures you do not run out of money too soon. This will involve taking a close look at your total income (investment income and non-investment income) and expenses, making assumptions about the future growth of your income and expenses, and deciding to what extent this demands drawing down your principal.

Not only will drawing down your principal reduce it over time, but investing in securities that decline in price will also be a way for your principal to lose value during retirement. When deciding the portfolio allocation that is right for you, one thing to consider is the risk to your principal based on the allocations you are favoring. This should be done with the awareness that no investment is completely risk-free. There will be varying degrees of risk at different periods of time.

The specific investment product(s) you choose can also have a huge impact on your principal. If you choose a bond fund rather than an individual bond, there could be dramatically different outcomes for your principal. If you want exposure to the oil industry, the investment vehicle you choose to gain that exposure could have a widely different outcome than another investment vehicle. For example, an exchange-traded product tracking crude oil prices could have drastically different returns from the stocks of a basket of companies in the petroleum business. Similarly, over time, a basket of stocks could end up with dramatically different returns from a broad market index. When you have decided the asset class allocation you would like for your retirement funds, you will then need to spend a significant amount of time choosing the specific investment products with which to gain exposure to those assets. Different securities may yield dramatically different returns.

Additionally, your principal could suffer the adverse consequences of being forced to sell securities to fund your expenses at a time when your investments are declining in value. Selling on weakness would, over time, compound the reductions in the principal, as there would be less money available for growth should your investments eventually rebound. Once again, the word used multiple times throughout this book comes into play: timing.

For the remainder of this chapter, I would like to focus on providing a few insights concerning portfolio allocation. I hope they will be useful when thinking through how to preserve the principal value of your retirement portfolio, both while in retirement and while building the portfolio on the way to retirement.

Invest in Companies, Not Just Stocks

If I chose 100 everyday investors and hedge fund managers at random and told each of them that I invested in Bank of America, I would likely get a variety of reactions. While each person might have a different reaction, I would venture to guess that the overwhelming majority of those 100 people would share one thing in common: They would assume that when I said I "invested in" Bank of America, I had purchased the stock. In a post-financial-crisis world in which a return *of* their money is for many investors more important than a return *on* their money, investing across a company's capital structure is something worth exploring.

Instead of spending all your time thinking about which stocks to buy and sending your bond allocation to a fixed income manager, consider the benefits of buying a company's bonds as well as its stock. After all, if you are sufficiently confident to buy the security at the very bottom of the food chain (common stock), why would you not have the confidence to buy a security toward the top (bonds)?

Rather than only focusing on whether a company's stock is worth an investment, take a look at whether your goals could be met by investing in multiple parts of that same company's capital structure. This might include preferred stock and convertible bonds. It might also include unsubordinated or subordinated bonds, whether secured or unsecured. Depending on the company, it may be possible to create a part-equity, part-debt allocation that provides reasonable income, reasonable inflation and deflation protection, and reasonable principal protection all at the same time. By doing a part-stock, part-bond allocation for a specific company, you would also change the level of liquidity and vary the level of principal protection compared with an all-stock allocation.

For example, if you have $20,000 you want to invest in a company whose stock is yielding 2.50% and whose long-term senior unsecured bond is yielding 4.75%, you can split the investment in any number of ways. Depending on how you allocate the money between the stock and the bond, you would change the upside price potential of the position, the level of risk to the principal, and the overall yield of the investment. By using 50% of your company-specific allocation to purchase the senior unsecured bond (with the intent to hold it to maturity) and 50% to purchase the stock, you create an average yield of 3.625% (2.50% + 4.75% = 7.25%; 7.25% / 2 = 3.625%). This would split the difference between the dividend yield of the stock and the bond yield.

By allocating 50% of the principal to the bond, you would reduce the overall volatility of the investment. Typically, over long periods of time, a corporation's bonds move in smaller price ranges than that same company's stock. Also, by allocating 50% of the investment to the bond, you have reduced the overall upside potential of the investment, but you have also provided more principal protection to the investment. The upside in the investment is limited by the fact that the bond will mature at par (assuming no default). A stock, however, theoretically has no upside price limitations. You have provided more principal protection and deflation protection because a bond will mature at par (assuming no default). A stock, on the other hand, could languish for many years and could potentially never return to the level at which you purchased it.

Even if the issuer of the bond defaults on its obligations, the bond allocation will provide an element of principal protection, given that there is *typically* far more recovery value on corporate bonds (especially senior bonds) than there is on company stock. Finally, with the bond allocation, you have also provided an element of income protection against the possibility of a company's cutting or eliminating its dividend. With a 100% stock allocation, you are at the mercy of the company's willingness to declare a dividend each year. By investing in that same company's bonds, you have put yourself in line ahead of the shareholders to receive an income stream from the company.

On the other hand, the 50% allocation to the stock provides upside to the investment that a 100% bond allocation would not provide. As previously mentioned, this is because there is theoretically no limit to the potential capital appreciation of a stock, whereas a bond matures at par. The equity portion of the allocation also provides the potential for increasing yields over time should the company grow its dividend. For example, if a company grew its dividend by 5%, compounded annually, in 10 years, the 2.50% yield on cost you started with would grow to 4.07%. This would change the overall yield on the allocation to 4.41% from the 3.625% you started with (4.07% + 4.75% = 8.82%; 8.82% / 2 = 4.41%).

This is an example of diversifying between asset classes (stocks and bonds) in a way many investors do on a market-wide level. Essentially, what investing across a company's capital structure does is allow you to diversify in a very specific way. You can choose asset class allocations for each company in which you invest as opposed to choosing them in a general market-wide way. You might choose a 50% bond, 50% stock allocation for half the companies in your portfolio and a 67% bond, 33% stock allocation for the other half. You choose the allocation based on your analysis of the company.

If you spend some time perusing a list of corporate bonds for some of the higher quality companies that issue debt, you may discover that the stocks of those companies have higher dividend yields than what their bonds are yielding. That has not been unusual during the era of ultra-low interest rates. But just because the bond is yielding less than the stock does not necessarily mean you should avoid the bond. When assessing the right asset allocation for an investment in a company, you will need to think through your risk tolerance, time horizons, future anticipated cash needs, and your views of the company's and the world's economic health. After doing so, you may decide that an allocation to the bond is worthwhile. Each investor's situation is unique; what may be right for one investor's portfolio may not be suitable for another's.

Target-Date Funds

If you are in the process of building a retirement portfolio, you may have come across a product called target-date funds. Over the past decade, there has been explosive growth in the use of target-date funds, especially in retirement accounts. Target-date funds are funds designed to automatically change allocations over time as investors near retirement. The funds are set up with a target-date attached to them that indicates the year in which investors are targeting retirement. As the fund approaches that date, it is supposed to gradually shift its allocation from "riskier" investments to more "conservative" investments. In the world of target-date funds, this means reducing the allocation to stocks while increasing the allocation to bonds and cash over time.

Also of importance, target-date funds are designed as funds of funds. A fund of funds does not hold stocks, bonds, or other securities directly, but it instead invests in other funds that hold such securities. Here is a basic overview of what theoretically happens behind the scenes when you invest in a target-date fund: First, you purchase shares of the target-date fund. Then, the target-date fund manager purchases shares of his fund's underlying funds (other mutual funds). And last, the fund managers of those mutual funds then take the money they received and purchase the securities underlying their funds.

If target-date retirement funds are the investing route you decide to take, keep in mind that you are not differentiating your portfolio in any way by investing in these funds. Target-date funds are a one-size-fits-all type of investment product. When you invest in one, you are basically putting your faith in the conventional wisdom that asset allocations should slowly shift from stocks to bonds and cash as you grow older regardless of financial conditions or valuations.

Determining your asset allocation solely based on your age is one investment idea that seems a bit off to me. What if the broader stock market were reaching new highs and trading at valuations typically associated with being extremely expensive? Should the investor in his or her 30s still choose the target-date retirement fund that would roughly correspond to his or her likely year of retirement? If so, such a fund would be heavily invested in equities. I would imagine that a broad market index trading at, say, 30 times earnings would eventually suffer the consequences of reaching that valuation. My guess is that would happen before the target-date fund chosen by the investor in his or her 30s ever shifted to a smaller equity allocation.

How about a scenario in which bonds, in general, were yielding more than 10%, inflation was falling, and the economy was showing signs of improvement? Should an investor in his or her 30s avoid a heavier allocation to those bonds, or might 10% yields on fixed income be high enough to increase the fixed income allocation of a portfolio?

Last, what about an investor 60 years of age who just watched the stock market and bond yields plunge to lows not seen in many years and concurrently notices an economy that seems to show some rays of hope? Should that investor be focused on lowering the allocation of equities in his or her portfolio, or might that be a good time to add to the equities allocation?

I recognize these are examples that might be characterized by some as a bit extreme. But they have all happened before and are certainly within the realm of possibility. Deciding your asset allocation based on your age alone completely ignores the fact that the financial markets might be indicating that you should do something different from what a target-date fund says you should do. Deciding your asset allocation based on your age seems like an investment strategy rooted purely in hope. Perhaps the strategy will work out. If it does, however, the success will be based purely on luck, rather than on having a well-crafted portfolio. Of course, there is always an element of luck involved when investing, but target-date funds seem to take the dependence an investor will have on luck to an entirely different level.

Cash Buffer

If you are already in retirement and juggling the difficult task of maintaining sufficient income to cover your expenses while at the same time trying not to draw down the principal of your portfolio too quickly, keeping a cash buffer may be quite helpful. By cash buffer, I mean uninvested funds that can be drawn on when your portfolio is performing poorly and you need money to supplement your income. It would be quite unfortunate to need to draw down your principal at precisely the same time the financial markets are going through turmoil. Selling some of your investments on weakness in order to fund expenses will only exacerbate the challenge of not drawing down your principal too quickly over time.

By selling when your portfolio is under stress, you will leave less money available for any potential rebound in asset prices that may come about at a later date. But by having a cash buffer meant to be accessed during times your portfolio is under stress, you will be able to avoid selling out of your securities at precisely the worst time. Ideally, you would then replenish your cash buffer by selling out of your investment portfolio after it has rebounded in price, thereby selling into strength rather than selling on weakness. In effect, drawing money from your cash buffer is like giving yourself a bridge loan. It buys you time until the financial markets recover.

* * * * *

In closing, principal preservation is an important theme for any investor building or managing a retirement portfolio. You should begin to think about principal preservation from the time you start accumulating assets for retirement and continue thinking about it through your retirement years. The more you are able to preserve and grow your principal during your younger years, the more helpful it will be when trying to make your money last through your retirement years. There will be times when focusing on preserving your principal may seem like the wrong thing to do. This can be especially true if financial bubbles are popping up all around you, and everyone else seems to be getting rich. But if you have a well-thought-out plan, and the plan is working, stick to it. Sometimes slow and steady wins the race.

Chapter 9

Miscellaneous Insights

As I mentioned in the introduction to this book, in order to feel as comfortable as possible in your retirement investments, you should have a good grasp of the decision-making process behind those selections. This is true whether you invest on your own or have someone else do it for you. Inherent in the decision-making process of building your retirement portfolio should be the following five fundamentals: predictable income, inflation protection, deflation protection, liquidity, and principal preservation. Now that I have discussed each of the five fundamentals of building a retirement portfolio, as well as a series of investment possibilities to consider, I will attempt to tie everything together. But before doing so, I would like to share several miscellaneous insights on investing.

One of the great difficulties of investing is sifting through all the news we read and hear regarding the financial markets, asset classes, and individual securities to determine what is worthwhile information. In addition to that, investors also have to grapple with the fact that our minds often lead us astray and succumb to a series of biases, which, if uncontrolled, can lead us to make very poor investing decisions.

Confirmation Bias and the Endowment Effect

As you invest over the years, continually ask yourself the following questions: Am I choosing to purchase certain assets because the facts suggest I should purchase those assets? Or am I choosing to purchase certain assets because my non-factual-based beliefs support my doing so? Do I first research and study an asset and then decide to purchase it? Or do I first decide to purchase an asset based on a preconceived notion or hypothesis, and then search for facts to confirm my preconceived notion or hypothesis? Do I give less weight to information that does not confirm my position and more weight to information that does confirm it? Do I ever end up owning an asset simply because I own it? Do I think an asset will go higher in price simply because I own that asset or because the fundamentals and financial market conditions support that asset going higher in price?

Confirmation bias is the tendency to favor information that supports your beliefs and to disregard or misinterpret information that does not support your beliefs. For example, perhaps you read an article full of anecdotal evidence that convinced you a particular asset class would soon be entering a bull market. You decide to research the matter for yourself. But because the article did such a great job convincing you of the merits of that asset class, you tend to favor information that supports the thesis behind investing in that asset class rather than giving equal attention to information that does not support the thesis. Or perhaps you do give equal attention to information that does not support the thesis, but you tend to misinterpret its true meaning.

Even after you already own an asset, biases still come into play in shaping your decision-making process. The endowment effect refers to the idea that people value something more than they otherwise would once ownership has been established. Think about all the great asset bubbles in history and what drove people to hold onto those assets even as prices were plummeting. Often times, the endowment effect can blind investors from seeing the true value of an investment. You may not realize that the asset you own has reached a level at which you think the price should still go higher, but others think the price is too high. The ability to recognize when an investment you have made has reached the point that it is no longer a value to most potential buyers is an important skill in investing.

You may be a shareholder in a company that will grow to become a very large player in its industry, but that does not mean the stock price of that company must continue to go higher over time. Cisco

Systems and Intel Corporation are two examples of companies that have grown into very large and very important players in their industries. Yet in late 2012, their stock prices are still nowhere near the highs they reached twelve years ago. Banks serve important roles in making sure credit flows to businesses and individuals and in making sure people's money is readily available for transactions. Yet in 2012, many of the largest banks in the world have stocks that have performed downright horribly over long periods of time.

Moreover, you may own an asset that has important uses in society, but that does not mean it must continue to rise in price over time. Houses serve an important function in society. Yet housing prices in many parts of the United States collapsed in recent history. Have you heard of people who are struggling to sell their homes because they refuse to sell at prices potential buyers are willing to pay? In some cases, this is because homeowners are underwater on their mortgages and therefore cannot afford to sell at lower prices. But in other cases, the homeowners are valuing their homes at above-market prices because the endowment effect is at work.

Perhaps you know someone who is an avid investor in investment products that track the price of crude oil. In the early 2000s, crude oil prices went ever higher, as investors wanted to profit from the belief in long-term supply and demand imbalances for oil resulting from a growing middle class in emerging markets. In 2012, the story can still be made of a growing middle class in countries such as China and India eventually driving crude oil demand to the point that supply will be unable to keep up. Yet in the summer of 2012, WTI light, sweet crude oil prices traded more than 40% lower than they did in 2008.

The front month WTI light, sweet crude oil futures contract is the price most often cited by the press in the United States as representing the price of oil. Concerning those investors who maintained long crude oil positions during those four years, there is a good chance that confirmation bias or the endowment effect contributed to the decision not to sell.

As you navigate the investing waters over the years, pay careful attention to how confirmation bias and the endowment effect may influence your decision-making. Also remember that just because there are persuasive opinions or facts that contradict your beliefs does not mean you must sell an asset. Do not be afraid to try to rip apart your investment thesis. Welcome opinions that are contrary to your own. Do not simply tolerate an opinion because it is polite to do so. Instead, genuinely welcome it because it gives you the opportunity to review why you believe what you believe and to decide whether or not it is time to adjust those beliefs. At times, it may be perfectly acceptable to ignore information that is contrary to your beliefs. After all, others are also susceptible to a variety of biases when forming their investment decisions.

Anchoring

Anchoring refers to the tendency to rely too much on one piece of information when making a decision. This overreliance on one piece of information can cause people to unknowingly adjust other inputs in the decision-making process to fit the framework of the anchor.

The investing world is not immune to anchors. In fact, the result of financial market participants falling prey to anchoring can even leave the door open for large inefficiencies in asset prices as well as portfolios failing to perform as expected. One example might be analysts releasing earnings estimates or price targets that have been influenced in even just the slightest way by the consensus forecasts. An analyst not looking to attract any unwanted attention might use a consensus forecast as an anchor from which to base his or her own forecast. The analyst might even do this subconsciously.

Another example of anchoring might be historic price-to-earnings ratios influencing your decision about whether an asset is cheap. Have you ever heard of "value traps"? A value trap refers to an asset that appears to be cheap based on historical averages of popular valuation metrics but in fact is not cheap at all. The market might be anticipating something of which you are not aware, making the asset appear cheap on a historical basis.

For example, you may think the S&P 500 is cheap because it trades at, say, 12 times earnings, and historically it trades with a price-to-earnings ratio in the mid-teens. But there may be factors at play that will keep the ratio low for many years to come. Therefore, if you purchase a security tracking the performance of the S&P 500, despite the fact that earnings may grow over time, a low and even falling price-to-earnings ratio could prevent you from ever realizing the returns you assumed you would.

A third, widely used anchor in investing is the purchase price of an asset. When you use the purchase price of an asset as an anchor against which to make further investment decisions, you risk subjecting yourself to a series of bad decisions. For instance, the purchase price of an asset may affect the price at which you sell an asset, despite the fact that the purchase price should have no bearing on what the optimal sale price is. This could lead you to hold an asset for far longer than you originally intended, which can bring with it a whole host of other consequences.

In the world of options, the purchase price of the underlying asset might determine the strike price at which a trader decides to purchase a put or the strike price at which a trader decides to sell a covered call. This can be true even if the strike price chosen is not the strike price that he or she would have chosen if the purchase price of the underlying asset would have been different. Incidentally, selling a covered call means you are granting a call buyer the right to purchase your shares from you at the option's strike price.

Becoming more aware of how cognitive biases influence your decision-making is an invaluable tool to pick up on your investing journey. It will help you to see things in a different light, help you to more objectively assess information being thrown your way, and hopefully lead you toward outcomes that are truly in your best interest. With this in mind, I would like to spend some time addressing the idea of buy-and-hold investing.

Buy-and-Hold

Please do not confuse long-term investing with buy-and-hold. Many in the financial industry use "long-term investing" interchangeably with "buy-and-hold." That is incorrect. In its simplest form, long-term investing involves having an investment plan based on your risk tolerance, time horizons, future anticipated cash needs, and views on the economic, political, and regulatory environments that is intended to help you achieve your financial goals. Your investment plan may include allocations you consider to be buy-and-hold that you intend to hold for many years. It may also include allocations you intend to keep for shorter periods of time. Long-term investors seek to use their investment plans to achieve their financial goals with an end date many years in the future. Buy-and-hold investing is one way people attempt to meet those financial goals as long-term investors. But buy-and-hold investing is not the only way to meet long-term financial goals.

Buy-and-hold as a strategy for achieving your long-term financial goals has become ingrained in the investing psyche over the decades. It solidified its place in the minds of most investors during the fabulous bull market of the 1980s and 1990s. In recent years, however, the merits of buy-and-hold investing have been questioned by some. Nevertheless, the financial industry continues to push buy-and-hold investing as the single best way to grow a retirement portfolio.

I am not seeking to change anyone's mind concerning buy-and-hold. But if buy-and-hold is your favorite style of investing and something in which you truly believe, then it should be able to survive an examination of the facts with respect to the returns investors have achieved over time using this strategy. Investors, as a collective whole, have become conditioned to believe that if they buy a security tracking the performance of a broad market index such as the S&P 500, over time, it will return compounded double-digit percentage growth on their money. And who can blame them for believing they will realize such returns? After all, over a 30-year period, from the S&P 500's bear market bottom at 101.44 on August 9, 1982 through its August 8, 2012 close, the S&P 500, on a capital appreciation basis alone (excluding dividends), had a compound annual return of just over 9%. That is quite impressive.

Let me pose a question: Did all the money you invested into the stock market since 1982 go into the market at precisely the time it reached its lows on August 9 of that year? If not, then the 9% plus compound annual return on a capital appreciation basis I referenced is not relative to your situation. In fact, I would bet that number has *no relevance to anybody*. Do you know anyone who went all-in at the lows on August 9, 1982, never made another purchase, and never took any withdrawals? Investors are routinely told about all sorts of time frames in which the broader market managed wonderful returns. I have even seen returns calculated back more than one hundred years. But are they relevant to your situation as an investor?

If you invest in individual stocks, historical broad market returns should be irrelevant to you. Even if a stock's beta is right around one, there are so many possible outcomes for a company's business over a multi-decade period that you should in no way rely on historical broad market returns as a guide for an individual stock's potential returns.

If you are someone who invests in broad market index funds, such as a fund tracking the S&P 500, what makes you confident the returns on your portfolio will repeat the 1982 to 2012 experience going forward? What if you are choosing points in time to invest that will deliver 1929 to 1982 type returns? From the 1929 high on the Dow Jones Industrial Average to the August 9, 1982 low, the Dow returned a meager 1.34% annually on a capital appreciation basis. Yes, you read that correctly. The Dow returned just 1.34% compounded annually, excluding dividends, over a nearly 53-year period. My reason for excluding dividends will be subsequently addressed.

Additionally, are you choosing just one moment in time to make your investment, never to add to the position again? If so, your timing will matter more than ever when trying to match 1982 to 2012 type returns. If not, you could easily end up doing far worse. Of course, you might end up doing far better as well. Various factors, including the timing of your investments, will determine that. Given that you have no way of knowing whether you are going all-in at a generational low in the broader market, why would 1982 to 2012 returns be of any relevance to you?

How many everyday people invest in the stock market via 401(k)s or some other type of defined contribution retirement plan that takes money from a paycheck and deposits it into the market every week, every two weeks, or once a month? According to the Investment Company Institute's (ICI) *2012 Investment Company Fact Book*, of the 118.7 million U.S. households in May 2011, 61%, or 72.4 million, participated in an employer-sponsored retirement plan. At the end of 2011, 40% of all employer-sponsored retirement plan assets, totaling $4.531 trillion, were in defined contribution plans.

Think about how many people you know who invest in the stock market mainly through a defined-contribution plan. At the end of 2010, 91% of all 401(k) participants in their 20s had exposure to equities. Among 401(k) participants in their 60s, the number of people with exposure to equities was still quite high (82%). Why should any of the people putting money into the stock market on a regular weekly, bi-weekly, or monthly schedule care at all about stock market returns quoted from one point in time?

I examined all week-ending and month-ending price levels for the S&P 500 from the week beginning Monday, August 9, 1982 through the subsequent 30 years. I wanted to see how a retirement portfolio into which contributions were flowing on a regular weekly, bi-weekly, or monthly basis would have performed during the period beginning with the onset of the great bull market of the 1980s and 1990s. I am not someone who came up with a hypothesis that buy-and-hold does not work and then cherry-picked a date to "prove" that point. Instead, I was curious what the returns were for people investing the way most everyday investors do in their retirement accounts during a period when the S&P 500 enjoyed spectacular returns. As previously mentioned, the S&P 500, without even including dividends, returned slightly over 9% compounded annually from its August 9, 1982 bear market low through its August 8, 2012 close. But did the typical investor's retirement portfolio, invested in the S&P 500, experience the same type of returns? It turns out the answer is *no*.

The following table shows the compound annual growth rate (CAGR) over a 30-year period for portfolios receiving equal dollar investments in the S&P 500 (via a security tracking the S&P 500's returns) beginning the last day of the week that the great bull market of the 1980s and 1990s commenced.

Table 9.1

	S&P 500 Cost Basis	Number of Contributions	CAGR
Contributions Made Every Week, Beginning the Week of 8/9/1982	777.127	1,566	1.995%
Contributions Made Every Other Week, Beginning the Week of 8/9/1982	776.851	783	1.960%
Contributions Made Every Other Week, Beginning the Week of 8/16/1982	777.403	783	1.994%
Contributions Made on the Last Day of the Month, Beginning 8/31/1982	777.176	360	1.931%

An investor putting an equal dollar amount into a security tracking the S&P 500 (like a mutual fund, for example) at the end of every week beginning the week of August 9, 1982 would have a cost basis of roughly 777 in S&P 500 terms during the summer of 2012. The same was true for the investor putting an equal dollar amount into the markets beginning the week of August 9, 1982 on a bi-weekly schedule and for the investor putting an equal dollar amount into the markets beginning the week of August 16, 1982 on a bi-weekly schedule. The investor making contributions on the last business day of each month, beginning August 31, 1982, and doing so for 360 consecutive months, also had a cost basis of approximately 777. The aforementioned cost bases assume no withdrawals were made from the investment account, thereby taking full advantage of the incredible heights to which stocks soared in the 1980s and 1990s. But with cost bases of roughly 777, those investors would have dramatically underperformed the S&P 500 over that 30-year period.

I was quite surprised to see the underperformance of money that was put into the market on a fixed schedule during perhaps the greatest bull market in history, followed by a decade of largely sideways price action (with a lot of volatility in between). From a capital appreciation standpoint, in all four scenarios, investors in the S&P 500 failed to achieve even a 2% compound annual return on their investment. How can that be? How could investors in each of the aforementioned scenarios end up with compound annual returns from capital appreciation of less than 2%? How could dollar-cost averaging, the strategy of buying into a security on a regular schedule, regardless of price or valuation, a strategy touted so highly by the financial industry, have failed so miserably?

It turns out that continuing to buy a market that only seems to go up is a good idea until that market stops going up. From 1982 until 2012, investors spent far more time buying stocks on the way up than they did accumulating stocks at low prices. While there were some vicious bear markets and pullbacks during the 1982 to 2012 time period, the sell-offs were short in duration. The lower prices from large pullbacks and bear markets did not last long enough to give investors putting money into the market on a fixed schedule sufficient time to accumulate tons of shares at lower prices. Instead, investors spent far more time buying on the way up, which continually raised their cost bases over time. The problem with a rising cost basis is that you need ever-rising prices to ensure that the new money you put into the market achieves the type of returns the original money achieved. And that has not happened.

As if the sub-2% returns are not bad enough, I have even more bad news for the retirement investor believing in indexing and buy-and-hold. I calculated the returns based on equal-dollar contributions rather than ever-rising contributions. But for many investors, nominal wages have been increasing since 1982, and with rising wages likely came rising retirement plan contributions. Not only were investors buying on the way up, but they were buying ever-larger dollar amounts on the way up. These rising dollar amounts varied depending on the investor, so there are literally millions of different scenarios that could be calculated to show the true cost basis for each investor. The point remains, however, that investing ever-greater amounts of money at ever-higher prices will produce a higher cost basis than would investing an equal dollar amount on a fixed schedule over time.

Even during the bear market of 2007 to 2009, a bear market that brought the S&P 500 down 57.69%, investors only had a short window of time to purchase shares at prices that would have reduced their cost bases. Therefore, despite the fact that contributions to a retirement plan in early 2009 would have likely been far greater from a monetary standpoint than contributions in the 1980s, they would not have helped to lower investors' cost bases by any significant amount.

In addition, if you were unfortunate enough to reinvest your dividends on top of ever-rising contributions, again, you were spending most of your time purchasing additional shares at ever-higher prices, thereby most likely contributing to a higher cost basis. What all this means is that the sub-2% returns previously mentioned are most likely the best case scenario. If you were continually purchasing ever-greater amounts at ever-higher prices, your cost basis is likely higher than the aforementioned 777, thereby reducing your overall returns even more.

To make matters even worse, the explosive growth of investing via a 401(k) during the 1980s and 1990s indicates that most 401(k) investors never had the opportunity to accumulate shares in the early stages of the great bull market. According to the Investment Company Institute's November 2006 *Research Perspective*, "401(k) Plans: A 25-Year Retrospective," the 401(k) was born on November 10, 1981. By the time the great bull market of the 1980s and 1990s began less than one year later, very few people were using 401(k)s. By 1985, approximately 10 million people were participating in 401(k)s, and that number kept growing, reaching 19 million in 1990, 28 million in 1995, and 40 million in 2000. More and more people were jumping on board the 401(k) train and plowing money into the stock market at ever-higher prices. So again, the compound annual returns I presented are likely *too high* for most people participating in the stock market by dollar-cost averaging through a 401(k).

Naturally, I would expect a few readers to be pulling their hair out while screaming that I excluded dividends from the total returns. There is a reason I excluded dividends. The dividend yield in 1982, 1985,

1990, or any other year is completely irrelevant to today's stock market investor since the dividend yield of years gone by is not the dividend yield of today. If an investor is trying to determine whether he or she should put *new* money into the stock market, looking at returns that include the S&P 500's 4% to 5% dividend yields of the 1982 to 1984 time period or the 3% to 4% dividend yields of the 1985 to 1991 time period does not make sense when today's dividend yield is hovering in the 2% to 2.25% range. Including those higher dividend yields would be disingenuous because people will not get those types of dividend yields on the S&P 500 today. A more honest way to assess historical returns from stocks is to first look at the capital appreciation portion of the return. Investors could then add the current dividend yield to the historical capital appreciation to get a more complete picture, all the while keeping in mind that the dividend yield will change over time.

Of course, as virtually any piece of investment literature will remind investors, usually in the fine print, past performance is not indicative of future performance. I will take this opportunity to say the same: Past performance is not indicative of future performance. In the future, your portfolio's performance might be far in excess of or far worse than the meager returns previously mentioned.

The purpose of my discussing returns for the typical 401(k) investor was to illustrate the following: When you hear about historical stock market returns that you might be using as an anchor for your expectations of future returns, make sure the returns quoted are relevant to your investing approach. Also, recognize that if dollar-cost averaging did not work for the typical retirement investor during perhaps the greatest bull market in history, it may be difficult for all your money invested over time to achieve the types of returns from equities that are all-too-often quoted by financial professionals.

Furthermore, it is important to understand that just because your account size has grown at a rate faster than the aforementioned sub-2% returns does not mean that the money you invested into the account has done so. Employer contributions can mask the returns of *your* contributions. Finally, the fact that investing in the S&P 500 did not work out from a capital appreciation standpoint does not mean that other stock market investments were not worthwhile. There were likely quite a number of individual stocks that provided tremendous returns on a capital appreciation basis and also kept their dividends at quite respectable levels.

And so I challenge you: If the often-quoted spectacular returns in the stock market are not relevant to your investing approach, then on what would you base the argument that buy-and-hold investing is the way to go? You may have a legitimate reason. I am merely trying to get you to think it through. If, after thinking through your investing approach and the relevance to you of the often-quoted historical returns for the S&P 500, you still think buy-and-hold is the way to go, let me add an additional challenge.

Answer each of the following questions: What will GDP growth be over the coming decades? What will capital expenditures, margins, and earnings growth look like for corporations over the coming decades? How much inflation or deflation will we experience over time? What levels will the national debt and state and federal budget deficits reach over the coming years? How much dividend growth should investors expect? What multiple will the broader stock market indices have year-by-year over the coming decades? How much growth in consumer spending should we expect in the years ahead? What type of wage growth will employees realize as time goes on?

I do not expect anybody to be able to answer these questions with any accuracy. I am simply trying to drive home the point that there are so many unknowns that will affect equity prices in the future. Putting your money into the stock market and using a buy-and-hold approach indicates that you have a level of faith that the unknown will work out in a way that drives stock prices higher over time. Buy-and-hold investors with multi-decade time horizons rely on hope that things will work out for the best. Hope is not exactly the best investment strategy. When hope is the cornerstone of an investment strategy, rather than just a small piece of the investment puzzle, there is a good argument to be made that the strategy is really just a form of gambling.

This discussion of buy-and-hold investing was not meant to try to convince you that buy-and-hold does or does not work. It was, however, meant to provide food for thought and get you to think about whether conventional wisdom is true. On a final note, to those who will never swear off buy-and-hold investing because of a belief that financial assets will sufficiently rise in price over the "long-term," I pose the following question: If buy-and-hold investing is guaranteed to work over an investing lifetime, for what do you need an investment advisor?

Secular Bull Markets

A secular bull market refers to various conditions that are in place to drive asset prices higher over a period of many years. There can be bear markets within a secular bull market, but the bear markets will not change the upward trend. The 1982 to 2000 U.S. stock market serves as an example of a secular bull market.

It is worth noting that the buy-and-hold mentality that is so widely touted in the investing community largely depends on the incredible returns of the 1982 to 2000 secular bull market in order to even have a chance of passing muster. I have already demonstrated the *irrelevance* of the often-quoted historical buy-and-hold returns. But for those investors who still believe buy-and-hold is the way to go, I would like to point out that many of the conditions helping to fuel the great bull market of 1982 to 2000 are not currently present. It does not mean other conditions cannot fuel a new secular bull market, but the onus is on the responsible investor to figure out what those conditions will be before blindly throwing money into the stock market.

During the 1982 to 2000 bull market, there was a long-term trend of falling interest rates that began at much higher levels than where we are today. Additionally, during that time period, there were very favorable consumer spending demographics. At the start of the bull market in 1982, the S&P 500's dividend yield was more than twice today's level. Also, at that time, the price-to-earnings ratio for the S&P 500 was in the single digits versus today's lower double-digit P/E ratio. Combine this with the current direction of credit standards (more stringent), the dependence of tens of millions of Americans on government transfer payments, anemic wage growth, and a job market struggling to provide an adequate number of full-time, well-paying jobs for the skill sets currently held by Americans, and you have to seriously question whether there is enough fuel for a new secular bull market.

Moreover, the legislative environment at the federal level has become so difficult to navigate that it seems to only breed uncertainty and confusion among individuals and businesses. Additionally, technology is advancing at such a rapid rate that it is pretty much impossible to know what the world will look like in ten years, let alone over the course of an investing lifetime or long retirement.

If a secular bull market is central to your buy-and-hold thesis, what do you see on the horizon to fuel a bull market comparable to the 1982 to 2000 experience?

Trusting Analysts

When conducting your research on various companies, you will likely come across analysts' opinions of those companies. Should you trust the price targets, ratings, and research provided by financial analysts? As you ponder this question, keep the following in mind:

1. There is an incentive for analysts not to stray too far from the pack when providing price targets and ratings on stocks. If you hang out with the crowd and are wrong, your reputation will likely remain intact, and you will likely get to keep your job. If, however, you veer off in your own direction time and time again and prove to be wrong, there is a good chance you will lose your job and damage your reputation. Beware of *groupthink* in the analyst community.

2. Analysts who want company executives to return their phone calls are certainly incentivized not to assign sell ratings to stocks. Furthermore, financial companies that wish to be considered for bond underwriting, mergers and acquisitions (M&A) business, or initial public offering (IPO) business certainly have incentives to impress upon their analysts the importance of keeping positive relationships with companies. Remember that incentives play a major role in business dealings and could have some influence on certain analysts' ratings.

3. If you believe that analysts provide completely truthful, unbiased research, price targets, and ratings, at least consider verifying their work.

4. Even if you do not trust analysts, respect the fact that they have the power to influence the prices of financial assets. This is true whether or not their opinions are trustworthy.

Random Musings

I would like to close this chapter with these random musings:

1. I have often heard that it is important to remove or suppress your emotions when investing. In my experience, when investing, it is better to *listen* to your emotions and to learn how to *manage* your emotions rather than suppress them. This is a process that can take a long time to master. The more actively engaged you are with your investments, the more emotionally challenging situations you will encounter. The combination of all sorts of experiences in the financial markets, as well as a conscious awareness of your emotions and an awareness of how you might react to various emotions under different circumstances, can help you get a much better grasp on investing.

2. Put aside your social and political beliefs when investing. While it may be admirable to stand up for that in which you believe, choosing an investment based on whether you agree with the social or political leanings of a company can easily turn into a recipe for disaster. Regarding economic beliefs, keep in mind that you may be correct in the eventual reaction of the financial markets to certain fiscal and monetary policies, but it may take far longer than you ever imagined for markets to reach that outcome. As I mentioned before, timing matters. Even if you are absolutely certain you will be correct in your assessment of the financial markets, and your assessment is based on your economic beliefs, you need to make sure that you can remain solvent longer than the markets can remain irrational in order to eventually profit from your points of view.

3. If your investing time frame is years, do not get caught up in the minute-to-minute and day-to-day movements of the financial

markets. Do, however, occasionally spend time reviewing the performance of your investments. It is important to make sure that your portfolio is performing the way you designed it to perform. If it is not, drill down to figure out why, and make a decision about whether the difficulty needs to be addressed or whether it will soon pass.

4. Do not marry an investment. You may be a "long-term investor," but that does not mean you cannot familiarize yourself with the sell button on your broker's trading platform. If the reasons you had for investing in a particular security turn out to be wrong, or the security ends up not performing the way you need it to as part of your overall portfolio allocation, then sell it. Do not let confirmation bias or the endowment effect convince you to continue owning something simply because you own it.

5. Spend a considerable amount of time constructing your retirement portfolio. Think about how much time you would likely spend during the entire process of purchasing a house. Spend at least that same amount of time, if not more, constructing your retirement portfolio. During the time you spend constructing your retirement portfolio, ask yourself lots of questions about the information you find. And when you are done asking questions, ask more questions.

6. Last, but certainly not least, do not let your ego get the best of you. A big ego can become your biggest enemy.

Part IV

Putting It All Together

Over the course of the last nine chapters, I presented a significant amount of information to digest. Whether you are in the beginning stages of building your retirement portfolio or at that point in your life when it is time to see what the portfolio is made of, I attempted to provide plenty of food for thought in this book. Now it is time to work on putting all that information together. I would like to help you organize your thoughts around the five fundamentals as well as the various asset classes and securities discussed in this book. But first, before ever being able to build a retirement portfolio, you will have to choose a company to act as custodian of your assets.

Chapter 10

Choosing a Custodian

of

Your Assets

If you invest for the future solely through your employer-sponsored retirement plan, you will likely not have to worry about choosing a financial company with which to set up an account until it is time to roll over your workplace retirement account into an IRA. Until that time, for better or worse, you will be stuck with the company your employer has chosen as custodian of your retirement assets. Other investors might invest their money in a non-employer-sponsored retirement account, such as an IRA. A third group of investors may choose to invest for retirement using a non-retirement account.

Whatever route you choose, at some point, you will likely need to select a financial company to act as custodian of your assets. There are so many possibilities from which to choose and no right answer when deciding which company is best. I would like to provide some insights based on my experiences and observations over the years.

1. If possible, open accounts with multiple companies. This may not be practical for some investors, but once you save enough money to avoid low balance fees and meet any minimum investment requirements, take the leap and open accounts with

multiple companies. As Lehman Brothers clients in 2008 and MF Global clients in 2011 found out, having your assets frozen because your broker went under is not a pleasant experience. This would be especially true if all your assets were with one company and it went under. Investors are taught to diversify their portfolios. Take diversification to the next level and diversify your portfolio across multiple custodians of your assets.

You may be tempted to think that one broker or one mutual fund provider combined with a deposit account at a bank would be sufficient. But when one of the custodians is holding your funds as bank deposits, you might end up holding far too much of your retirement portfolio in cash. Having two custodians that allow you to invest in many of the types of securities discussed in this book as well as a bank account to boot will help ensure that your retirement funds are not forced to be overly exposed to cash when attempting to diversify across custodians.

Make sure at least one of the companies you choose is the custodian of large numbers of retail accounts, has a well-established name in the investing world, and unbelievable sums of money under management. By unbelievable sums of money under management, I am envisioning at least a few hundred billion dollars. This should help protect you in the event that your brokerage firm goes under.

If you put yourself in the same boat as many millions of other everyday people, and your brokerage firm is on the verge of failing, your situation is quite likely to attract the attention of lawmakers. When brokerage firms with a small number of clients or smaller amounts of money under management have their assets frozen, people in positions of power will not care as much as they will if millions of people have their assets frozen and cannot pay their bills. There is no way for me to prove this. But I contend that if your broker goes under and your assets are frozen along with the assets of millions of other everyday people, the government will force a quick resolution, even if it ends up being through a temporary workaround.

2. Do not forget to assess fees and commissions across all the asset classes in which you are interested in investing. Do not

necessarily choose one broker over another just because the commission on the equity side of the business is more favorable. You could have one broker charging you a few dollars less per equity trade but a few dollars more per bond purchased. Think through how many transactions you would generally expect to make over certain periods of time across different asset classes, and calculate a rough estimate of the total commission charges. This will help make the commission comparison across brokers a bit easier.

In terms of stocks, in today's day and age, you should not pay more than $10 per trade. And remember, that is the high end of the range. At this time, I am not willing to manage the equity portion of my portfolio for $10 per trade. But for people doing very little buying and selling in the portfolio, a $10 trade here or there is probably acceptable if there are other parts of that custodian's offerings that balance things out.

When it comes to *stock* commissions, you may find that some brokers charge far less than others. One broker may charge $8 per trade while another charges $2 per trade. It may be tempting to give the company offering $2 trades the lead for your equity business because, after all, a $6 difference per trade can add up. But the company charging more might be known for getting better executions on client orders. For example, a company that seems to have the ability to consistently get clients sub-penny fills may be the better choice over a company that offers lower commissions but cannot get you better executions. Sub-penny fills refer to orders that are executed at a fraction of a penny. If you enter a buy limit order at $10.00 when the bid-ask is $9.99 by $10.00, and you get filled at $9.997, that would be an example of sub-penny fill. It would also be an example of a broker's getting you a better execution due to access to hidden liquidity (refer to Chapter 7 for more on "hidden liquidity").

If a broker seems to consistently have access to what I refer to as "sub-penny hidden liquidity," it may be worth choosing to do business with that broker. After all, the benefit of buying at slightly cheaper prices can certainly offset the slightly higher equity commissions. When searching for a company to act as custodian of your assets, talk to a customer service representative about executions on stock orders. If the representative seems confused by your question, that may be a good indication as to whether that company considers order execution a priority.

Regarding commissions on *options* trading, comparing companies by the flat rate they charge per contract is insufficient. In addition to the flat rate per contract, companies typically charge an additional fee, which usually equals the standard equity commission for one trade. This means that although two companies may charge the same flat rate per options contract, the total commissions will be different. For example, let's say companies X and Y both charge $0.75 per options contract. Company X, however, charges an additional $8 per options trade whereas company Y only charges an additional $5 per trade. Therefore, company X will actually charge you more per options trade than company Y will despite both companies having the same flat rate fee per contract.

Additionally, do not forget to look at whether a company charges for exercising options and for option assignments. Some companies will only charge a commission equal to the standard equity commission for these services whereas other companies may add additional per share or per contract charges. So, once again, there could be two companies with similar flat rate fees per options contract but drastically different end results for charges to the customer.

In terms of commissions on *bonds*, nowadays, there is no need to pay more than $2 per bond, and there are several brokers now offering the opportunity to trade for $1 per bond. Furthermore, if a broker is advertising no commissions on bond purchases, this should be a red flag that the broker marks up bonds before selling them to you. Bond markups are very common, and some can be quite egregious. Perhaps the worst part about them is that clients often do not know they are overpaying to the extent they are because a markup is built into the price at which the broker sells the bond to the client.

There are two ways you can check whether you are receiving a fair price or are being sold a bond at a price far above what the market is currently selling it for. The best way is to check the current offers in the market. If you do not have access to this information because your broker does not provide it to clients, you can check the most recent trades on a bond to see if they are anywhere close to the price your broker is advertising. The Financial Industry Regulatory Authority, better known as FINRA, provides a detailed breakdown of bond trades, by CUSIP, on its website.

An example of a bond markup is as follows: Your broker is trying to sell you a bond from its inventory for 100 cents on the dollar. The bond is currently being offered for 98 cents on the dollar in the secondary market. If you purchase 10 bonds (1 bond = $1,000 face value) at 100 cents on the dollar, it would cost $10,000. If you purchase 10 bonds at 98 cents on the dollar, it would cost $9,800. The 2 cents on the dollar markup (also called a 2 point markup) would cost you $200 more than what the bond is being offered for in the secondary market. If you bought that same bond from a broker charging a $1 per bond commission, you would just pay $9,800 plus a $10 commission.

Another example of a markup is as follows: You ask your broker to purchase a particular bond for you that is not currently in that broker's inventory. The broker goes to the secondary market and purchases the bond for 100 cents on the dollar but charges you 101 cents on the dollar. On a $10,000 face value purchase, that one point markup equals $100. Compare this to a $10 commission if you were charged $1 per bond. How common are 1 or 2 point markups? I see them all the time when I sift through trade data for bonds. In fact, I have seen plenty of markups in excess of 2 points.

One final note regarding bond commissions: Be sure to check what the minimum commission is per bond trade. A broker may be offering a commission of $1 per bond, but if the minimum commission per trade is $10, then you must buy at least 10 bonds to get the $1 per bond commission.

3. Learn about the investment research each custodian makes available to its clients as well as the investing software clients have access to. Also, pay attention to the stipulations that come with accessing such research or software. In particular, with respect to investing software, you may have to have a certain amount of

assets with your broker or trade with a certain frequency to gain full access to the best software.

4. Customer service matters. By "customer service," I am not necessarily referring to whether the person on the other end of the phone is the nicest person in the world. Rather, I am more specifically referring to the ability of the company's representatives to fix problems with customer accounts and to fix those problems within a reasonable amount of time.

Rating customer service is, of course, highly subjective. Scouring the internet for reviews of financial companies can be handy. I do not want to recommend any specific website for providing excellent reviews because, quite frankly, I do not know each website's business relationships. When it comes to websites ranking customer service, I would want to know about any conflicts of interest before making a recommendation. Using a search engine and keywords such as "broker review" and "broker survey" is a good starting point for research on customer service in the investing world.

After choosing one or more financial services companies with which to do business, you will have to fill out the paper work to open your account. If you are interested in investing in financial products beyond mutual funds, be sure that the paperwork you submit includes a brokerage account agreement. In addition, if you are interested in options trading, you will need to fill out the options agreement and designate the level of options trading approval you are seeking.

Once you have an account set up and funded, you will be able to start making purchases. The question is, what should you buy? To help answer that question, I will try to help you organize your thoughts within the framework of the five fundamentals described in this book: predictable income, inflation protection, deflation protection, liquidity, and principal preservation.

Chapter 11

Ranking the 5 Fundamentals

The first step in figuring out which assets to accumulate in your retirement portfolio is to think about how important each of the five fundamentals is to you. Start by ranking each one according to its importance to you today, keeping in mind that your opinion can change as time goes on. If you are 25 years old and beginning to build a retirement portfolio, one particular fundamental may be less important to you now than it will be when you are 65 and beginning to depend on the retirement portfolio for income.

A retirement portfolio is a fluid creation that should adapt to the needs and wants of the portfolio's owner in the context of an ever-changing economy and market structure. You need not be locked into the investments you initially choose. Sometimes there is a bit of trial and error involved in creating an ideal portfolio. Approach the ranking of the five fundamentals according to their level of importance to you today, taking into account whatever visibility into the future you believe you may have.

_____ Predictable Income

_____ Inflation Protection

_____ Deflation Protection

_____ Liquidity

_____ Principal Preservation

Once you have ranked each of the five fundamentals in terms of its importance to you, the next step is to rank each of the investment vehicles and assets mentioned in the predictable income, inflation protection, and deflation protection parts of the book. I am going to leave Social Security benefits, Railroad Retirement benefits, and defined benefit plans off the list since those are income streams you cannot purchase in the financial markets but instead will either receive or not receive based on your employment history. You should, however, keep in mind a rough estimate of how much you expect to receive from those income streams when thinking through how to construct your retirement portfolio.

Also, there may be other income streams not mentioned in this book that will provide you income during retirement. You should certainly add those into your plan as well. One source of income mentioned in passing in this book is a part-time job. For people content with a "working retirement," a part-time job might help to plug any holes in the retirement portfolio's ability to generate sufficient income. An investment vehicle I have not yet mentioned is a Business Development Company (BDC). BDCs are publicly traded entities known for investing in smaller companies. They are sometimes compared to venture capital or private equity because of the types of companies in which they invest.

Additionally, peer-to-peer (P2P) lending is another source of income some investors might want to consider. P2P lending has experienced explosive growth in recent years, specifically through the companies Lending Club and Prosper.com. These companies offer investors the opportunity to browse through loan listings from people seeking loans for a variety of reasons. By lending money through Lending Club or Prosper.com, investors can bring in much higher yields over much shorter time frames than they can through other investment products in today's ultra-low-interest-rate environment. With that said, it is very important to note that there are numerous risks with this type of investment, including the unknown of what would happen to your investment in the event of a Lending Club or Prosper.com bankruptcy.

Also, despite choosing the people to whom you will lend money, you are not making direct loans to the people requesting the funds. Instead, you are lending money to Lending Club or Prosper.com and are issued a note in return. Think of a note in the same way you would think of a bond. When you are issued a note by Lending Club or Prosper.com, the company has made a promise to repay you based on the terms of the loans you made to people through the company. There are plenty of other things worth understanding and considering before venturing into the world of peer-to-peer lending. I highly recommend reading the prospectus for Lending Club and/or Prosper.com before investing with either of these companies.

Now let's get back to the ranking activity. The following items are presented as one large list rather than broken down by predictable income, inflation protection, and deflation protection. I did intentionally leave "Dividends from Equities or Equity-Like Investments" and "Fixed Income Products" *on* the list despite subcategories of those larger topics being included on the list as well.

Rank the following 32 investment vehicles and assets according to how you envision your retirement portfolio looking today in the context of planning for the future. Investment vehicles and assets that will be part of your retirement portfolio should be ranked higher than those you are less certain about and those that will definitely not be part of the portfolio. It may be helpful to organize these on a separate sheet of paper.

_____ Annuities

_____ Dividends from Equities or Equity-Like Investments

_____ Fixed Income Products

_____ Real Estate Investment Trusts (REITs)

_____ Master Limited Partnerships (MLPs)

_____ Gold

_____ Silver

_____ Platinum

_____ Copper

_____ Diamonds

_____ Dividend Growth Stocks

_____ High-Yield Bonds

_____ Commodities, excluding Precious Metals and Copper

_____ Companies in Industries from Which You Believe Inflationary Pressures Will Arise

_____ Foreign Companies Declaring Dividends in Their Local Currencies

_____ Companies with a Global Presence

_____ Variable/Floating-Rate Bonds

_____ Foreign Currency Denominated Bonds

_____ Out-of-the-Money Call Options

_____ Foreign Currencies

_____ Real Estate

_____ Art

_____ Cash

_____ Treasury Bills, Notes, Bonds

_____ High-Quality Investment Grade Corporate Bonds

_____ Zero-Coupon Bonds

_____ Convertible Bonds

_____ Stocks with Yield Support

_____ Stocks of Companies Selling Things People Need (i.e. consumer staples, utilities, major drug manufacturers, health care, etc.)

_____ Low Beta Stocks

_____ Buying and Selling Put Options

_____ Stores of Value

After you have ranked the investment vehicles and assets mentioned in the predictable income, inflation protection, and deflation protection sections of this book, it is time to look for anomalies in your rankings. For example, is inflation protection at the top of your five fundamentals ranking but the top of the investment vehicles and assets ranking is nothing but investments geared toward deflation protection? Or are you most concerned about predictable income in the five fundamentals ranking, but the assets you ranked the highest are gold and zero-coupon bonds, which do not provide income streams? Perhaps you ranked fixed income products as a top priority but then ranked every type of fixed income investment as a low priority.

Also, incorporate principal preservation into the search for anomalies by comparing where you ranked it under the five fundamentals versus the types of assets you ranked at the top of the longer list. If principal preservation is a top concern of yours, but fixed income products are toward the bottom of your list while copper is near the top, you will want to reevaluate your rankings.

Let's now bring liquidity into the mix. Take a look at the various investment vehicles and assets you ranked in the top quarter to top third of that list. These are the investments you feel are most likely to be incorporated into your retirement portfolio. Look at these investments one-by-one, and think about *how* you would like to gain exposure to each of them (individual securities, ETFs, futures, etc.). Do this while keeping in mind where you ranked liquidity in the five fundamentals ranking. This is where you may find some anomalies.

For example, if high-yield bonds are near the top of your list, you will have to consider whether individual bonds or bond funds are right for you. A high-yield exchange-traded fund is likely to provide more liquidity than many individual bonds. Therefore, if liquidity is a top concern of yours, you might lean toward a bond fund.

Should dividends from equities be near the top of your potential investments for a retirement portfolio, you will have to choose between traditional mutual funds with that exposure, exchange-traded products with that exposure, or individual stocks. If you ranked liquidity toward the bottom of the five fundamentals list, you may be more inclined to go with mutual funds. Mutual funds do not allow for intraday trading like exchange-traded products and individual stocks do and therefore make them less liquid in terms of an investor's ability to get the exact price he or she wants at the exact time he or she wants it.

After completing your search for anomalies and tweaking your rankings based on the anomalies you found, it will be time to decide the types of investments to include in your portfolio as well as the allocations to each of those investments. Naturally, you will want to focus on the investment vehicles and assets that are toward the top of your rankings. There is no definitive number I can offer in terms of how many different types of assets you should have exposure to or what percentages to assign them in your portfolio. I would, however, encourage you to keep the portfolio as *simple* as you possibly can without compromising a portfolio structure that will encompass the five fundamentals and help you work toward your goals.

Also, when constructing the portfolio, remember that it is not necessary to go all-in, buying full positions in every asset all at once. A well-constructed retirement portfolio may take years to construct as you slowly build positions over time, waiting for the financial markets to provide you opportunities to purchase the assets you want at attractive prices. Of course, the amount of time you have to build the portfolio will also be partially determined by your age. If you are on the verge of retirement and, after thinking through the rankings you completed, discover that your portfolio does not encompass the diversity and type of allocation you want, you may have to speed things up and start buying quickly.

For those readers not on the verge of retirement, I would encourage you to complete the exercise previously outlined a second time. But instead of approaching the rankings from how the retirement portfolio should be constructed today, think about how you will want it to look on the day you retire. After ranking everything a second time, compare the results with those from the first time you completed the exercise. The differences between the two will help you realize the type of portfolio shifts you will need to make over time. Even if you plan to have a financial advisor take charge of your portfolio, the information you glean from these exercises will be useful not only when selecting the advisor, but also when communicating with the financial advisor about what it is you want him or her to do with your money.

After deciding the types of investment vehicles and assets to include in your portfolio, it will be time for individual security selection. I mentioned earlier that relying on hope as the cornerstone of an investment strategy, rather than as a small piece of the investment puzzle, would make the strategy akin to a form of gambling. This is true even if your time frame is "the long-term." If you are not sufficiently confident in your security-selection abilities to move the crux of your investment strategy beyond hope (there is always a little hope involved), you may want to find a financial professional whose investment strategies are not deep-rooted in hope to manage your money for you.

After it has been decided which specific securities you want to purchase for your retirement portfolio, but before you actually purchase them, you should consider calculating the annual income your portfolio will generate based on those securities. Then, add this income to any other sources of income you will have, such as Social Security, a pension, a part-time job, etc. Next, calculate what will be left over after taxes are accounted for, and compare that number to your projected annual expenses. If your after-tax income is less than your projected annual expenses, you will have to either increase your income or cut your expenses.

In order to increase your investment income, you will likely have to increase the risk of your portfolio's holdings. If you are inclined to do so in an attempt to generate more income, make sure you do not increase the risk to an extent that the portfolio will cause you too much stress. Given the low-interest-rate environment of recent years, some investors may feel compelled to move into what are typically considered riskier securities in search of higher yields. Before you do this, consider the negative side effects to your health that might accompany taking on more risk with your money. If your portfolio is causing you tremendous amounts of stress on a daily basis, consider reexamining the holdings to figure out why and work to eliminate the stress inducer(s).

Should you decide that increasing your income to bring it in line with your expenses is not a viable option, you will have to take a serious look at cutting your spending. This is true at any point in your retirement. Perhaps you started out with income that was sufficient to cover your expenses, but as prices marched higher, your income did not keep up. When after-tax income is not sufficient to meet your spending levels, and you cannot figure out a way to increase your income, you will eventually have to look at cutting spending.

* * * * *

Building your ideal retirement portfolio can be a daunting task. There is no single best portfolio allocation and no foolproof strategy for ensuring investment success. I did not write this book to overwhelm you or make you believe you need to hire an investment professional to manage your money. But it is important to recognize the scale of building a well-rounded retirement portfolio. It will take a lot of time and a lot of serious thought. It is not something that should be done overnight. At the same time, if you decide to manage your money yourself, you are likely to learn a lot and maybe even find some enjoyment in it.

Regardless of whether you choose to take control of your portfolio or delegate the responsibility to a money manager, I hope you find the contents of this book useful in helping to make you a better-informed investor.

Good luck and happy investing!

Index

About the Author

The Financial Lexicon has spent nearly a decade in the financial world and has extensive experience trading and investing in equities, options, fixed income, and alternative investment products. If you would like to read more by The Financial Lexicon, visit SeekingAlpha.com or LearnBonds.com.

Made in the USA
Lexington, KY
18 June 2013